A User's Manual
for Living in the World

A book about personal empowerment

by George Constantinidis, Ph.D.

CRAZY HORSE BOOKS

Cover Art by Julie Allen

Edited by Merry Markum

Contents

In our sleep, pain which cannot forget falls drop by drop upon the heart until, in our own despair, against our will, comes wisdom through the awful grace of God.

- Aeschylus

Some men see things as they are, and ask "why?" I dream things that never were, and say, "why not?"

- George Bernard Shaw

Dedication

For Devon; for Ryan, Kevin and Kelly; for Joy; for Clark, David, Elyssa and Elizabeth; and for Julie and Bree Lynne. All of you represent our highest hopes for a future of harmonious enlightenment.

For Popi, Tassos, Basil, Merry, Mick, Jimmy, Bobby, Jeff, Brandy and Rodie, who provided me with some out-of-this-world inspiration!

For Christina, who taught me more about unconditional love than any human I ever encountered.

About the Author

Dr. George Constantinidis has been a practicing psychotherapist for over twenty-five years. He has worked in both non-profit and corporate mental health facilities, as well as his own private practice, with clients from diverse backgrounds and varied presenting problems. His clients have included teen runaways involved in the drug and prostitution underworld of New York City, court-mandated sexual offenders, AIDS patients, victims of sexual abuse, substance abusers, and people in troubled relationships.

Social and political issues began to attract George's attention and invite his participation while he was still a high school student in the late 1960's. The decade's four important political assassinations, as well as the increasing involvement of the United States in an unpopular and costly conflict in Vietnam, invited him to become active in political campaigns and anti-war protests. Like many others in his generation, George sought remedies for the country's ills in the political process. Among his other activities, he worked in the Bedford-Stuyvesant area of Brooklyn as a volunteer for Robert Kennedy's presidential campaign in 1968. Senator Kennedy's assassination, and the subsequent violence at the Democratic Convention of 1968 in Chicago, caused him to doubt the utility of his participation in the political process as a meaningful way of producing social reforms.

George was influenced by the works of Albert Camus, R. D. Laing and Albert Ellis, which he first encountered as a college undergraduate, in deciding to pursue the study of psychology and psychotherapy. However, his pursuit of psychology as a field of study and a profession has also left him with the disturbing impression that the profession suffers from the same extreme dependence on the scientific method and the same lack of spirituality and lack of regard for the individual person that plagues many of our other social institutions.

More recently, George has discovered an affinity with the writings and ideas of Deepak Chopra, Louise Hay, Wayne Dyer, Stuart Wilde and Leo Buscaglia, as well as the inspiring books of Richard Bach, Marianne Williamson, Pat Rodegast and Neale Donald Walsch. It is George's belief that these authors are at the forefront of a new era of spiritual awakening which will revolutionize human existence on Earth.

George was a founding member of the Legacy Counseling Center in Dallas, Texas, and its first volunteer counselor. Today, Legacy provides hundreds of hours of free counseling per month to people infected with HIV, as well as their families and loved ones. He believes that his work with the terminally ill provided him with a deeper and more profound education about life, death and the nature of human existence than all of his professional and academic training and experience combined.

After indulging his love of writing with occasional articles and contributions to various publications, George has realized a long-held ambition by completing his first book, *A User's Manual for Living in the World*. It is drawn from his personal and professional experiences from a quarter-century of working both within and outside the mental health establishment, and represents his reflections on our society, the nature of our existence, and his ideas of how to get the most out of our time on this planet.

Acknowledgment

People who are willing to admit that they are acquainted with me over any length of time frequently describe me with these adjectives (at least, to my face): opinionated, irreverent, perceptive, passionate, contentious, supportive. There are other descriptions of me, of course, but, like me or loathe me, you are not likely to be spared my views on most aspects of life once you have come within the sound of my voice.

Expressing my views in my usual blunt and sometimes caustic manner has, on occasion, cost me jobs, relationships, promotions, and opportunities. This tendency towards unvarnished expression has also gained for me enduring friendships, passionate loves, and the invaluable experience of participating in the furthering of some very worthwhile causes. Still, until now, I have never had the impulse to express myself publicly at length about the many and varied aspects of life I have been fortunate and privileged to experience. Never, that is, until the impulse to write this book came along.

It would be accurate to say that I did not write this book. It wrote itself. Although I had entertained vague fantasies about doing it, I had never attempted to write a book before; yet, one day, I sat at the keyboard of my computer and composed, like some demented caricature of Vladimir Horowitz pounding on his piano keys, until exhaustion overtook inspiration. This scene repeated itself almost daily, for well over a year. Although my day-to-day life continued, the book became my central focus, my passion, and my creation. It *compelled* me to sit and write it, and to edit, rewrite and refine it, like a proud and doting parent grooming a gifted child. (When I sent the manuscript off to be professionally edited, I felt like a father watching his child being wheeled into a hospital's operating room.) It comes from an unnamed place deep within me, and gives voice to many thoughts I had never articulated or inter-related before—as well as many I never knew I held, until I saw them expressing themselves in the text. I belong to this work much more than it may be said to belong to me.

When the inspiration to start writing first came to me, I was at a very difficult point in my life. I was sharing my home and life with Merry, whom I loved very much, and who was at the time battling a cancer that was gradually invading more and more of her body, and causing her virtually unrelieved and extreme pain. Our resources and energies were primarily devoted to the relentless battle against this disease, which would claim her life less than a year later.

Merry and I found some relief from the disease's impositions on our life in spending long hours walking arm in arm and talking, among the natural beauty around our home, in between trips to the hospital and another of many radiation or chemotherapy treatments. We discussed and explored the many applications and ramifications of the ideas and concepts that formed the basis for our shared belief system, which had been a great part of our strong attraction to one another in the first place. It was while sitting on a boat dock on Nassau Point in the pre-dawn mist, watching an orange-red sun slowly rising over the tree line on Shelter Island and reflecting on a mirror-still Peconic Bay, that Merry interrupted my rambling discourse on my thoughts about some matter that occupied us at the time with a suggestion: "Why don't you write a book about all this?"

I was taken aback, because I had never thought about writing a book. Oh, sure, on occasion I had contributed articles and letters-to-the-editor to various publications; but writing was something I did for amusement and primarily for private consumption, in between seeing clients at my office and doing "real work." As I was articulating this objection, my real reservation about writing such a book occurred to me, and I shared it with Merry. Who was *I* to talk about the meaning of life, to tell others how to live and what's important? My own life seemed a parade of failed relationships, unfinished works, erratic finances, questionable decisions, regrettable behaviors, people I'd let down and disappointed, and situations I wished I'd handled differently. If to err was human, I was as human as anyone I knew!

Merry brought me out of this quagmire of self-deprecation in an instant, as only she could. With a kiss on my cheek, she reminded me that all of my perceived limitations were the lessons and experiences that had brought me to the awareness of the insights that I shared with her, and that had formed the basis for the deep personal bond between us. What's more, I had forgotten that all my alleged inadequacies were actually the gifts that had contributed to my growth and awakening. She encouraged me to share with others, in writing, what I was discovering within myself. In fact, she pledged to see to it that I made time to write even a little bit in the book every day. She committed to read and edit my text, and, true to her word, devoted herself to this task daily, often in the midst of considerable pain, until her disease took her away from me.

Thanks to Merry's inspiration and guidance, the text was gradually filled in—an amorphous, incoherent mass at first, that gradually began to take form into sections and chapters later. The book, indeed, had a life and momentum of its own, and continued to write itself through me. In fact, sometimes it would raise me out of bed in the middle of the night, or tear me away from a mid-day reverie, so I could return to writing some new thought, insight, or awareness in it. In the process of its creation, I experienced incredible self-realization and growth, as well as the revelation that what we can all access within us is so much greater than what we perceive ourselves to be, given the assumed limitations of our human awareness.

Merry provided the inspiration and early direction for this book, and helped me decide on its format and content. If the old saying that "behind every great man is a good woman" is true, I have been blessed far more than most. I hope and trust that I am at heart a good man, but I was beyond a doubt blessed with the companionship, love, influence and guidance of a *great* woman! Her influence is present throughout this work, and has transformed the entire book into an entity truly deserving of the label "labor of love."

Well, here it is, Blondie! Thank you!

Introduction

This is a book for and about people who want to stand up for themselves, reclaim their personal power, and rediscover their innate capacity to heal themselves. In the process, those who read this book and internalize its message will come to understand and accept that the capacity to recover their personal power and independence has been theirs all along, and the awareness of that ability has been subtly but effectively drained from them by a societal structure and a system of scientific philosophy that promotes a view of the common person as a helpless victim of powerful external influences. A legal system skewed to protect the wealthy and control the poor, a scientific and anti-humanistic medical establishment which enriches the practitioners at the expense of the manipulated patient, and a political system that espouses equal representation while creating a forum which permits plutocrats to dominate and exploit the masses are all manifestations of a society which has long ago abandoned any interest in the welfare of its common citizens, relegating them instead to the role of expendable commodities. Readers will understand how and why this self-serving societal structure promotes dependency, addiction, helplessness, and a total loss of personal aware-

ness; and, in recovering their sense of self and self-empowerment, will be able to better understand, analyze, and effectively
overcome the societal influences contributing to their mystification and dysfunction.

Back in the 1960's, R. D. Laing wrote that "we are all
functioning in a post-hypnotic trance, induced in early childhood." What is also true is that there are societal institutions
specifically designed to keep us in that trance, and to deny us
access to original thoughts, our innate healing and renewing
energy, and ultimately the discovery of the wonderful, complete, divinely inspired beings that we all are. Nowhere is the
mystification of the self more evident than in the very institutions that are supposedly designed to aid and support us in
becoming whole on a physical, emotional, and spiritual level.

I have worked for well over twenty years as a clinical
psychotherapist, both in private practice and in institutional
settings. My clients have included juvenile delinquents, drug
and alcohol addicts, teen prostitutes, so-called "career criminals," abused and battered spouses, sexual offenders, AIDS
patients, and the criminally insane. I have worked with—and
often against—psychiatric hospitals, religious organizations,
volunteer centers, the courts, the "corrections" system (a gross
and horribly misleading misnomer, if there ever was one!), and
government bureaucracies. In my experiences are included
some very gratifying successes, as well as some crushing and
maddeningly frustrating setbacks. Through it all, I have earned

some hard-gained wisdom: we have surrounded ourselves with an imperfect world, one in which people and institutions don't always act according to their stated purpose, which are designed to take advantage of the individual's weaknesses and insecurities so as to keep us all a part of the same herd, believing the same myths and feeling contented with the same carefully controlled morsels.

The greatest threat to this system of mass exploitation is the awakening of the individual person, and the unleashing of the creativity, fulfillment and sheer joy of life each and every one of us is capable of and has within us. It is my hope that this sharing of my thoughts and my anecdotal experiences, as well as the call to awaken and recover the awareness of each of our divinely inspired selves, will be another modest contribution to the massive spiritual awakening that is apparently already emerging in our culture. In so doing, I want to acknowledge the mentors who have contributed to my own awakening process, and whom I consider my spiritual parents: Scott Adams, Stacey Allen, Richard Bach, Molly Behannon, Berke Breathed, Leo Buscaglia, Taylor Caldwell, Albert Camus, George Carlin, Jimmy Cartier, Deepak Chopra, Wayne Dyer, Bob Dylan, Albert Ellis, Kahlil Gibran, Allen Ginsberg, Bob Gold, Whoopi Goldberg, Louise Hay, Siri Hutcheson, James Hillman, Gary Jordan, Jack and Bobby Kennedy, Martin Luther King, Marti Kranzberg, R. D. Laing, Timmy Lawton, Martine Maiorana, Merry Markum, Jim Marrs, Jimmy

Measley, George Orwell, Carol Philbrick, John Reed, Pat Rodegast, Robert Romanyshyn, Oliver Stone, Sallie Stratton, Charlotte Taft, Gene Trimboli, Garry Trudeau, Jan Hendrik van den Berg, Mike Vandewater, Yogeesh Wagle, Neale Walsch, Stuart Wilde, Robert Williams, Robin Williams and Marianne Williamson.

I know some of you personally, and closely enough to have shared my innermost thoughts and feelings with you. Others I know through your writings, recorded teachings, and artistry, which have moved me to laughter, tears, and a feeling of absolute love for life and all in it. All of you are very special to me, and represent for me the finest possible interpretation of the term "divinely human." I am also deeply grateful and amazed to see how many of you have blessed my life; your very numbers overwhelm me, and help me appreciate how fortunate I have been!

Thank you all for your footsteps along my path!

Chapter 1

Society and Sociopolitical
"Norms" (and Cliffs)
(With apologies to the cast of "Cheers"...)

Society, from the most primitive aboriginal village to the most sophisticated 20th century nation, has as its primary purpose the organization of its members in a system deemed to be most beneficial to the whole, but not necessarily to the maximum benefit of each individual within it. All current complex societies have a strong element of totalitarianism within them, no matter which political system they officially espouse. By this I mean that in all societies, including our own, the benefit of the group is valued above the benefit and potential development of most individuals within it. This is just as true in a small village as it is in a nation of hundreds of millions. The more developed and sophisticated the society, the more this is the case—whether we're talking about "communist" dictatorships or western "democracies." Notice that I said the benefit of the group is deemed to be above the benefit of *most*, not *all* individuals within the whole. Most societies are also oligarchies, with a ruling elite that uses its economic leverage, as well as its political and judicial power, with the consent and complicity of business and religious institutions to control events and trends so as to maximize the advantages of the ruling elite. Anyone living in one of the western "democracies" who really believes that the individual, with the clear exception of the select few (to be found in the United States on lists such as the Forbes 500 or Who's Who), has any influence on social policy and direction or the selection of political leaders, is profoundly deluded.

In the preface to her best-selling novel, *Captains and the Kings*, Taylor Caldwell dedicated the work to the young, whom she wanted to inform about the true nature and operating manner of world government. She warned them that, regardless of appearances of voting procedures and "due process," the operations and policies of the world's governments are controlled by a small group of wealthy elite. This select group of wealthy men manipulates world events, controls national leaders (who are its functional employees), and organizes wars, economic trends and upheavals, coups d'etat and assassinations. It has no national, political, or religious affiliations or loyalties, and focuses solely on the further accumulation of power and wealth for its members.

Caldwell's book became a best-seller and a television miniseries, but this most important part of her message—and her main motivation in writing the book—was conveniently omitted from the television presentation, and is not always published along with the body of the work. Her message about the powerful who control the course of history, and who are perpetuating the delusion of popular rule while reserving control of governments and events for themselves behind the scenes, has become obscured.

One area in which the disparity between the powerful wealthy and the masses they control is obvious is in the application of "justice" within our courts of law. Even a cursory examination of our court system reveals one standard of liability before the law for the wealthy, and another for the average person. In my own lifetime, the acquittals, minimal sentences or outright lack of official investigation in the cases of Klaus von Bulow, Senator Ted Kennedy (at Chappaquiddick), President Richard Nixon, Patty Hearst, and Leona Helmsley reveal the disparity of "justice" in America between the privileged wealthy and the rest of us. Besides the economic disparity, there is also a racial disparity in the manner that our society dispenses "justice" in our courts, which is referred to more extensively in the discussion on the inordinately high proportion of minority prisoners in our prison system later in this chapter.

Our government, as a representation of the collective unconscious of our society (and boy, is it *ever* encouraging our collective lack of consciousness!), participates in this process of collusion, deception and mystification. The "powers that be" bemoan the tragedy of overspending in social programs, while overspending in absurd and unnecessary amounts for a defunct and overbloated military establishment. We are loath to give a welfare family an extra 25 dollars a month, especially if it's a minority family, with little political influence; but we spend, without hesitation, hundreds of dollars on a hammer or a toilet seat for the armed services.

A recent edition of one New York City newspaper ran side by side two stories which illustrated the absurd priorities and gross bias which shape our socioeconomic policies: one story detailed a government plan to crack down on those who default on student loans, making it more difficult for thousands of needy students to finance their college educations in the future. The program was expected to save the government about twenty million dollars over the next eight years, by making student loans less easily available, at the cost of denying higher education to many deserving young people in the future. Right alongside of this story ran another about Congress approving the production of a new fighter airplane, which was not deemed necessary by military experts, but was nonetheless superior in performance to the planes currently in use. Over one hundred such planes had been ordered, *at a cost of about $22 million per airplane!* In other words, the savings from the student loan cutbacks over the next eight years had been spent one hundred times over in one day for an airplane we don't even need! However, the new and very costly airplanes would bring a boost to the economy of several states and congressional districts, also boosting the careers of the politicians who approved this appropriation. On the other hand, poor students have little political clout, so their needs could be easily sacrificed at minimal risk to the politicians' interests. With priorities as warped as these, is it any wonder our economy lags behind those of many other industrialized nations, or that our students compare so poorly in performance to those of Japan and western Europe?

We are sold on a government "of the people, for the people and by the people" that allows 95 percent of the wealth to be concentrated in the hands of less than five percent of the population. The oligarchy that controls policy and governmental changeovers, including the selection of "viable candidates" in national elections, does so without any meaningful effort to advance the lot of the average person, or of exploited minorities. Finally, there is no protest about a government that consents to the replacement of its designated leaders by violent, decidedly undemocratic overthrow and assassination in a supposedly democratic society. Transition through political murder is routinely blamed on "lone nuts," the reported assassins, whose publicized ideology is exactly the opposite of the factions ordering the radical shift in power and benefitting from its consequences. This public symbolic hanging of the alleged perpetrator is a sacrifice to protect the real instigators and their motives.

Abraham Lincoln was assassinated by John Wilkes Booth. No wider conspiracy was reported, even though two of Lincoln's cabinet members were almost simultaneously murdered in other parts of the city. Lincoln's assassination, by a supposed "Southern sympathizer," in fact cleared the way for the economic rape of the South following the Civil War by the victorious Northerners, in contradiction of his proposed policy of "malice toward none, and charity for all" in the Reconstruction period. The assassin was trapped and shot to death by soldiers soon thereafter, thus avoiding his testimony in a criminal trial.

Just a little less than a century later, a decidedly pacifist and one-world president, John Kennedy, promoted removal of U.S. forces from Vietnam, along with cooperative exploration of space with the Soviet Union, in contrast to a competitive "space race." These controversial decisions came in the aftermath of Kennedy's bypassing a golden opportunity to initiate World War III, contrary to the strong urging of his own military advisors, in the Cuban missile crisis of 1962. Kennedy further antagonized military and political conservatives by becoming the first American president to declare civil rights a moral issue, committing the government's resources to guarantee equality among all races and religions. He was assassinated less than a year later, supposedly by a Marxist sympathizer who, it was later revealed, just happened to be on the payroll of the FBI and CIA. The alleged assassin was also murdered soon afterwards, so he'd never have the opportunity to defend himself in a trial, and possibly expose the actual plotters. The beneficiaries of these acts were the militant right-wingers and munitions manufacturers who exploited Kennedy's death to expand the war in Vietnam, and escalate the "Cold War," ultimately resulting in the Soviets' invasion of Czechoslovakia in 1968.

Finally, a darling of the American right wing, Richard Nixon, was driven from office by the Watergate scandal—not coincidentally, after attempting to reduce the scale of the Cold War between the United States and the communist superpowers, establish diplomatic relations with Communist China, and end the Vietnam War. At least, Nixon may be said to have been more fortunate than Kennedy in one respect, because at least in his case the ruling establishment was satisfied with *character* assassination. What our government says it is pursuing, and what it actually promotes, are very different policies. Woe to whomever stands in the way of the power elite behind the scenes.

Society promotes policies and ideas in order to further its aims, with little regard for the interests of the common person, and does so by promoting conformity as a very desirable quality—perhaps *the* most important for an "average citizen." People are told and encouraged to believe what political ideas to hold, what lifestyle patterns to adopt, what career and life goals to aspire to and pursue, what products to consume and acquire. This is accomplished with the acquiescence and compliance of most persons within that group, persons who have succumbed to the social conditioning and mass hypnosis which establishes what is "normal" and "acceptable." It is facilitated by the manipulation and exploitation of basic feelings of insecurity commonly present in the majority of people among us, those who have yet to examine and develop their own intellectual potential and their inner connection to their spiritual or "higher" self. A sense of relief for people's insecurity and feelings of inadequacy is provided by giving them a sense of belonging to a greater whole, with which they can identify and in which they can find a sense of empowerment and protection against common enemies. This "greater whole" to which one can feel he or she belongs can be one or more of a number of groups: The middle class, suburbia, caucasians, Southerners, the Rotary Club, Orthodox Jews, Republicans, "people like us"—all of these are examples of labels for exclusive affiliations one may assume.

Hitler was well aware of the power such illusions of mass empowerment have over insecure and desperate people. He united and controlled a war-torn and economically devastated Germany to a great extent by focusing the German people's energies against perceived outsiders such as "non-Aryans" and Jews, and in the process forged a society with formidable economic and military power.

Somewhat more subtle, but equally effective and coercive forms of self-delusion, are present in our society today. They serve to unite the insecure "us," or "real Americans," against "them," minority groups within our country, or other nations and cultures. The vast majority of people are, unfortunately, more than content to remain intellectually lazy, spiritually undeveloped, and otherwise unassertive. They readily accept what is presented to them as "normal," and pass from cradle to grave trying to remain within those "safe" but intellectually and spiritually numbing parameters. They permit the printed media, "talk radio" programs, and television discussion shows to decide for them what is "normal," what is "good for them," and what is "moral" and "proper." The media also employ survey results and opinion polls to further indicate to their followers what the prevailing trends within society are, and what the person must conform to in order to fit in. In the process, the media often create the very trends they purport to be reporting to us.

We are bombarded daily with directives from the establishment about "what's good for America," the various political factions' plans for the next several years and decades, coercive "suggestions" for future business and employment trends, etc. While this is going on, we get megadoses of beliefs and standards of "morality" that attempt to define and restrict our thinking and behavior patterns within limits that make us easier to manage, classify and control. Supporting the political parties in power (and their policies) is "patriotic;" presenting alternative political and social options is "subversive." Accepting beliefs like the importance and value of concepts such as the inherent goodness of hard work, the inevitability of the triumph of justice over inequity, and the desirability and pursuit of material comforts is considered character-building, as well as "good for all Americans;" condemning those living in alternate lifestyles, such as homosexuals, people in interracial relationships, and those in unconventional professions (especially those not primarily driven by a high profit motive), is labeled moral, and so are racism, sexism, and the imposition of the standards and beliefs of one religious sect on others in the name of preserving "traditional values!" In recent times, it has become fashionable to use euphemisms such as "conservative" or "traditionalist" to describe people espousing racist, sexist, and homophobic views, thus removing the stigma from such viewpoints and presenting them as legitimate alternatives to non-discriminatory perspectives. Conversely, supporting unrestricted creativity in children, questioning the value of established religious and social norms, and pursuing spirituality through unconventional belief systems is labeled at least "irresponsible," or more likely "destructive to the social fabric." Supporting the right of people to choose whatever living arrangement or level of social interaction they are most comfortable with, especially as these choices deviate from what is considered normal and moral, is to be immoral and perverted.

In some people's minds, it is worthy of literal elimination from the societal "body."

Along with these moral and behavioral restrictions comes the promotion of a series of behavioral patterns and material goals which keep the individual mired in the swamp of societal hypnosis, conducting oneself and pursuing goals that keep far too many persons among us stuck on the treadmill of "accomplishment" and "climb up the societal ladder," at the expense of inner awareness and spiritual development.

We are encouraged to stuff our bodies with high-fat, high-cholesterol, sugary, salty and preservative-laden foods that promote lethargy and disease, such as fast-food hamburgers, sugar-and-preservative laden "snacks" and packaged foods, and greasy, fatty chips and cakes with little nutritional value, but greater risks to our health. Further, we are encouraged to learn to like such foods as these, to consider them special treats, and view occasions to consume them as special opportunities. Conversely, those promoting healthy nutrition that includes eating mostly fresh fruits and vegetables are considered by the social mainstream to be health nuts, cultural whackos, humorless fanatics who have gone too far in the extreme pursuit of physical health and good nutrition.

There are many scientific studies showing that red meat is a nutritional booby trap, laden with saturated fats, growth hormones and additives that help line the pockets of the food industry at the expense of the consumer's health. This does not inhibit the beef industry from promoting the consumption of red meat as an indicator of "real masculinity"—witness the advertisements in which the popular actor James Garner promoted beef as "real food," ironically just before he underwent cardiac bypass surgery. Eating red meat has been politicized in the media as the "right" of every American to consume "traditional fare" at the dinner table, even if that fare promotes diseases such as cancer and heart ailments, restricts energy and activity levels, and shortens life. Conservative defenders of the business establishment, like talk-show hosts Rush Limbaugh, Michael Reagan and G. Gordon Liddy, routinely promote eating red meat as an act of asserting one's loyalty to traditional values, and the avoidance of such a practice as an implication of a lack of masculinity and patriotism. Similar critiques can be made in the case of other popular foods, which remain popular thanks to constant and heavy promotion by a food industry motivated more by profit than serving the public interest, including eggs, butter, sausage, and bacon.

We are further encouraged to purchase and consume indisputably harmful substances that make no pretense of having any nutritional value, that are so damaging to one's health that they must carry warning labels to the potential consumer. These are promoted and consumed at staggering rates nonetheless, with monetary profit to the manufacturers once again taking precedence over the consumer's health and welfare. In the face of spiraling cancer, addiction, and disease rates, alcohol and tobacco consumption are promoted in advertising as lifestyle-enhancing practices, indicative of a person's sophistication, social dexterity and sexual attractiveness—the earned and deserved rewards of hard work and success.

The American government provides generous subsidies for tobacco farmers, while hypocritically pretending to be restricting advertising and sales of their product. Perhaps this is viewed by some as one of the many necessary compromises in reaching a consensus between conflicting politically powerful factions in a society; however, once the veneer of a democratic government dissolves, the conclusion must be that the establishment obfuscates its intent to support economically powerful concerns by issuing impotent warnings and restrictions "in the public interest," in order to conceal its own impotence and reluctance to affect real changes. In any case, such "restrictions" obviously have little effect: In the face of conclusive research proving the devastating health hazards of tobacco use, smoking among American adolescents has risen to epidemic proportions.

In the case of beer advertisements, the assumed link between consumption of beer and one's tendency to participate in sports and an active lifestyle is heavily reinforced in advertising. I defy you to name *one* important sporting event on television that has not been sponsored, at least in part, by at least one major brewery! The implication is that, even if you have no athletic talent whatsoever, you can still *appear* to be athletic and, by inference, virile and sexually attractive by being seen consuming a beer. Other alcoholic products, as well as tobacco goods (why are they called "goods," when they're so bad for you?) are promoted as indicators of social facility, sexual appeal and sophistication, and the rewarding sources of pleasure in compensation for one's efforts, demanding lifestyle, and contributions to society.

Can you imagine saying to someone that in order to show your appreciation for his hard work and efforts you'll give him some poison to put in his body? We haven't overtly said that to anyone since Socrates. Yet, that is exactly what promoters for tobacco and alcohol products do through their advertising—without ever emphasizing their products' very dangerous properties, of course!

All this is very ironic in a society that, in stark paradox to its economic interests, pretends to promote a "war" on drugs and to encourage its young to "just say no" to addictive substances. The incredible amounts of funds spent on law enforcement and efforts to control the illegal drug trade are themselves a criminal waste of funds and manpower that have admittedly had little effect on the distribution of illegal drugs and the spiraling rates of addiction, especially in the inner cities and among the poor. These resources could be much better used to establish and enhance community programs that would make drug use less likely and attractive, as well as provide better treatment for the addict. Putting a fraction of the funds committed to legal prosecution and incarceration of drug users into rehabilitation and educational programs would be a much more effective and efficient method in limiting the use of drugs. However, continuing on the present course maintains the illusion that some effort is being made by the authorities to control drug abuse, even though just about everyone connected with the attempt to control drugs in this manner *admits* the ineffectuality of such methods. They continue for two reasons: They give the illusion of good will and a desire to protect the citizenry on the part of government (along with keeping a significant portion of the police and military occupied and employed, thus justifying their budgetary expenditures); and, they continue to permit drugs to permeate and ravage the "undesirable" segments of society—the poor and the minorities—while also keeping them sufficiently medicated to ensure their lack of resistance against the status quo. In addition, tacit permission for drug trade and consumption within minority communities not only limits the opportunity for educational and economic development within these groups, but also permits law enforcement to periodically "harvest" a portion of the members of such subcultures, thus effectively limiting or controlling their numbers, as was the case with the proles in George Orwell's prophetic novel, *1984.* In American society, the proliferation of African-Americans and Hispanic-Americans among the prison population has reached scandalous proportions; it is currently estimated that one in four black males in America between the ages of 20 and

40 has participated in the "corrections" system—either as a prisoner, parolee, or on probation! Over 80 percent of such offenders are linked to the illegal drug trade at some level.

Along with tobacco and alcohol, Americans are encouraged to consume drugs like caffeine and artificial sweeteners in a variety of forms, as well as a staggering amount of prescription and over-the-counter medications for manipulating one's affective states and behavior patterns through artificial means, at a horrendous toll to that person's system. We are by far the most medicated nation in the history of the world, with drugs readily available to wake us up in the morning, put us to sleep at night, relieve our feelings of stress and anxiety, and provide us with relief from every uncomfortable feeling we can ever have or imagine. This instant chemical gratification and relief is accomplished at great expense: Not only does it reinforce in our subconscious that we have no control over our body and mind, and must seek help from the pharmacist in controlling and regulating our moods and behavior; we are also encouraged to medicate ourselves right out of our awareness and self-empowerment. We become chemically controlled automatons, content to get through the day or week as out of touch with our uncomfortable feelings as possible, even if that also means losing the connection to our inner self and our awareness of our Higher Self. That's a horrifyingly high price to pay for the palliatives of conformity and temporary comfort.

Social conformity and separation from our inner awareness is also accomplished through less physically manipulative means, which are no less mood-altering or sedating. The phrase "keeping up with the Joneses" has been a treasured and oft-repeated cliche' of American society for decades; the principle persists, and influences our focus and life decisions in so many ways. We are encouraged to pursue certain levels of income through whatever means necessary, in order to have access to the material luxuries that we have been persuaded make life worthy of our participation. If, in the process, we indenture ourselves to pursuits that require the devoting of great segments of our waking hours and efforts, so much the better. Such occupations earn us the additional social status of "hard worker" and "good provider," while taking even more time away from the opportunity to realize our true selves and enjoy communing with those we love. The greater truth we are encouraged to ignore, that pursuing one's true life purpose will produce happiness, life satisfaction and abundant wealth with effortless ease, is withheld from most of us in our social indoctrination. It would probably be dismissed by most among us at least as "unrealistic," or at the most as subversive or heretical. The majority among us go on in mindless pursuit of higher salary, more status, and more material acquisitions, by way of affirming our status and "success," without stopping to "smell the flowers along the way," and consider what the true meaning and purpose of our life might be. The pursuit and acquisition of faster cars, older whiskey, larger houses, younger lovers all seem to get in the way of discovering our true purpose in life—which may be why they are all never quite enough in the long run. The whole distracting, dysfunctional materialistic mess is tersely summed up by a slogan found on some bumper stickers: "He who dies with the most toys, wins!" It's as if life was no more than a grand Monopoly game, with no purpose other than mindless, endless acquisition.

Materialism is yet another way to medicate us, perhaps the ultimate addiction to deflect our attention from fulfilling our true purpose in life and fulfill the spiritual mission that inspired our incarnation. You can be certain that people who gravitate to you because they become primarily aware of your material comfort will not be available to you for a personal relationship in the truest sense of the term, even though they may come to live with you. This is because they will not have connected with you at the true personal level that lies beyond external appearances and the world's illusions.

My paternal grandfather used to say, "people who marry for money earn every penny of it." While it is true that everyone who pursues their life's mission will be happy and will lack for nothing, material or otherwise, it is also true that such ease and abundance comes as a result of being "on purpose," not as a goal in and of itself. Remain true to your purpose and mission, what Deepak Chopra calls "dharma," and you will lack for nothing in life—certainly not in life satisfaction. How do you know when you are on purpose? Easy: you will never work again a day in your life! That's not to say that you won't be productive, or won't contribute to the enhancement of others' lives; in fact, you'll probably be a profound influence to a great many people who cross your path. You will influence their lives, and they yours, towards far greater happiness, fulfillment and awareness. What I mean by not ever working again is that you'll be so immersed in your life's purpose, and will so enjoy participating in its processes day in and day out, that you will not feel any anxiety, strain or effort—the sensations that typically accompany our concept of "work." If you're not sure how to arrive at this state, or to be sure that you are in it, I will provide you with a complete description and guidelines in the subsequent section of this book concerned with choosing work and vocations. In the meantime, the encouraging admonition to "do your own thing" that was coined a couple of decades ago seems to encapsulate the idea very well. Go do your thing; you'll be rewarded handsomely for it in more ways than one! You'll also be happier than you ever dreamed you could ever be while attempting to conform to others' expectations.

There was a gap in our experience in this century that did indeed expose us to the benefits of individual development, acceptance and promotion of alternative lifestyles. There was widespread rejection and condemnation of a society based on materialism and violence, and a virtual flood of originality and artistic expression. All this occurred in the decade of the 1960's, and the generation that was at the forefront of this cultural and spiritual revolution, my generation, was forever altered by its own initiatives and heightened awareness. That generation conclusively demonstrated that rejection of the sociopolitical agenda of the military-industrial complex and its replacement by a culture of peace, love and expanded awareness could produce an atmosphere of harmony and creativity that was unimaginable before. Those of us who remember participating in anti-war protests, "love-ins" and days-long concerts like Woodstock have been shown the capacity to peacefully coexist and to discard the many damaging "isms" of traditional society: racism, sexism, etc.

The seminal event of the decade, the music festival at Woodstock, demonstrated that half a million people can live within a relatively crowded space without police or military supervision, and live out the concepts of peace, harmony and love without externally imposed and complicated codes of conduct, or the need for enforcement and punishment of any kind.

It's true that the initiatives of the 1960's were subverted from within by excessive drug use and an emphasis on indulgence, and by the expanding of sexuality and expression beyond intimacy and creativity. In the process, we trivialized our relationships to one another, and to our own higher self. Our best leaders were assassinated, imprisoned, or encouraged to assimilate back into traditional society. We lost Dr. Martin

Luther King, the Kennedy brothers, and Malcolm X. Many of our most prominent activists found sanctuary in law and business schools, Washington's political labyrinth, or the morass of Wall Street. The two subsequent decades were marked by a reactionary turn to materialism and a "me-first" mentality, that served to return us to the soul-numbing selfishness and greed so identified as an integral part of "the American dream" by previous generations. The "leaders" that emerged in this era ranged from the power-hungry and corrupt (Nixon), to the benignly incompetent (Carter), to the unaware and unquestioning (Reagan), and to those politically entrapped by the system and their own political ambitions (Ford and Bush). But from this reactionary quagmire has emerged an underground movement that returns to and builds upon the spiritual awareness initiated in the 1960's. This movement is not violent, and it has constituents that are politically liberal and conservative, rich and poor, black and white, male and female. It has grown in awareness beyond the 60's beliefs that the world can be transformed through politics and economics, or from within a hopelessly corrupt and entangled system. We recognize the naivete and frustration inherent in attempting to reform a society from within its own self-serving institutions, while it continues to cling to its own ineffective and violating methods: violence and coercion. Reluctantly, we have come to recognize and accept that, as George Carlin says, the power elite have "bought, sold and paid for this country a long time ago." As this realization set in, our naivete and attendant political activism from the early '60's has been transformed to commitments and initiatives of a different sort. Instead of volunteering for the Peace Corps (which the more cynical among us suspected had quickly evolved into a branch of the CIA), and for working on the electoral campaigns of candidates like Eugene McCarthy, Robert Kennedy and George McGovern, we have turned towards and discovered a new mission in spirituality and the human potential movement. It is no coincidence that the type of candidate that inspired our imagination has also disappeared from the political scene, replaced by pale imitations like Gary Hart, or outright caricatures, like Jimmy Carter and Ronald Reagan. We no longer wondered what our country could do for us, or we for it; the bitter reply to that inquiry was all-too-obvious.

We have discovered among ourselves a reliance on our spiritual awareness and focus on our Higher Self that is fundamentally altering the nature of human experience on our planet. This groundswell has already produced the sweeping political changes in eastern Europe, changes that were unimaginable only a few years before they occurred. These changes in the collective awareness resulted in the toppling of "communist" dictatorships and the destruction of the Berlin Wall, as well as the timely emergence of enlightened leaders such as Anwar Sadat, Vaclav Havel, Yitzhak Rabin, and Mikhail Gorbachev. (Remember, there are no coincidences!) It has produced the basis for common societies beyond national boundaries, economic and cultural coalitions among large numbers of nations, and the virtual elimination of military institutions among most of the civilized nations (an area in which the United States still lags behind, sadly). We have witnessed the reconciliation of centuries-old feuds among ethnic groups in conflict, as has occurred among the Israelis and Palestinians, as well as many traditional European antagonists, most notably the French and Germans.

Some might argue that the trend towards demilitarization around the globe is made possible *because* of the existence of a strong American military presence. However, the sweeping changes effected in Europe and the Middle East without American military intervention, as well as the ineffectiveness of the American army in attempting to produce permanent peaceful changes in places like Iraq, Lebanon, Bosnia and Somalia make such a position difficult to support. It is more apparent that apologists for a strong American armed force share a view of an economy largely reliant on military expenditures. This is the same perspective that led to the expansion of the Vietnam War and the Cold War in the 1960's, and that led to the economic collapse from within in the Soviet Union. Those who fail to learn the lessons of history are condemned to repeat them.

The world based on disclaiming the existence of the spirit is quickly being passed by. The reductionist, impersonal schools of scientific thought that liken the human heart to a mere pump which can be repaired or replaced like any other mechanical part, that liken the wonder of the rainbow to simple refracted light, and the moon of lovers to a mere mass of minerals orbiting through space are falling by the wayside. In their place has come an awareness of the greater Intelligence connecting and harmonizing all beings and functions within the Universe, an Intelligence that is more pervasive and awe-inspiring than any of our conceptions of "magic."

Those of us who recognize the divinity of the spirit and the capacity of the heart to feel and heal have moved beyond the reliance on intellect alone, or even primarily, as the interpreter and definer of human experience. We have moved beyond the sterility of statistics and computer data to the expansion and appreciation of the multifaceted nature of our awareness. In the process, we are bearing witness to the dissolution of the old exploitative, paternalistic and violent Piscean age, leading into the Aquarian era of maximizing human potential and expanding spiritual awareness. It is a movement that is geometrically expanding in intensity and influence, and the traditionalist establishment is powerless to stop or even contain it, as its experiences in eastern Europe have already demonstrated.

We have come to an age where a belief in magic, the capacity to visualize and manifest life as we desire it, is beyond the realm of fantasy. It is the recognition and affirmation of the power within us all to effect remarkable transformations in ourselves and our environment. We have come to recognize the limitations of our reliance on external institutions and the limited, outmoded potential of our science, religion and philosophy, and are learning to accept the unlimited power of the Divinity within us. We are learning that the questions we addressed outside ourselves have their answers within, and that we have unlimited capacity to effect our body, our relationships, and our world if we tap into that divine spark within us. In order to do so, we need not rely on any government, expert authority, or spiritual guru. Within each of us are all the answers we seek, and the resources we require. To paraphrase that esteemed philosopher, Pogo, "we have met the Messiah, and he is us!" In order to access them, we need only remember that affluence is so much more than the absence of poverty, health much more than the absence of disease, peace much more than the absence of conflict. We are ready to move beyond society, beyond history, beyond materialism, simply by recognizing and developing our connection to the divine spark within us as well as accepting and nurturing that same divinity in one another. The resulting explosion of spiritual transformation is about to alter human experience on earth to a state of bliss far, far beyond our current limited imagination.

Chapter 2

A Lie We Have Agreed Upon:
Racism and Discrimination
in the American Experience

Studs Terkel has called it "the American obsession." Racial discrimination, division and conflict have been central to the American experience since early colonial times, and persist to this day. Racial discrimination affects our economics, politics, social agendas, and our very image and future as a nation which sometimes aspires to be considered the moral policeman and guide for the rest of the planet. It is continually covered up and officially ignored, in favor of myths and lies about equality and the "level playing field" into which American society has supposedly been transformed. In spite of these lies and mis-representations, discrimination and inequality repeatedly rise up to confront us with our attempts at self-deception, like the alcoholic uncle who repeatedly embarrasses us by staggering into our dinner party. From Woodrow Wilson, Warren G. Harding and the Ku Klux Klan to Amos 'n Andy, from Jackie

Robinson and Rosa Parks to Rodney King and O. J. Simpson, our ingrained racism rises to remind us that equality and equal opportunity are as absent from our society as ethics are from our business and government. Racism is the nightmare in the midst of the American dream, the bogeyman that awakens us to the ugly reality of the continued exploitation of one race by another, to the detriment of all.

Not surprisingly, history texts tend to gloss over or completely obscure the pervasive presence of racism in American history, which also obscures the links between racist policies and the manifestations of inequality and abuse in our societal structure. A significant effort in reversing this policy, and unmasking the influence and effects of racism on American society and culture, was made by Dr. James W. Loewen, a former professor of history at the University of Mississippi. In his revealing book, *Lies My Teacher Told Me*, Dr. Loewen cites the following in demonstrating the central influence of racism within the American social fabric:

Long before the establishment of the United States as a nation, life on the North American continent was influenced by the uneasy merging of the native American, black, and white races. Native Americans, of course, had inhabited North America for at least 12,000 years before the arrival of caucasians and Africans in the sixteenth century a.d., according to estimates by archaeologists and anthropologists. As soon as the other two races arrived, a pattern was set which continues to our times:

The white race pursued a pattern of attempting to exterminate the native Americans (and largely succeeding, in numbers that dwarf the mass murder of European Jews and gypsies by the Nazis during World War II), and exploit the Africans through slavery and discrimination (overtly until 1865, somewhat more subtly but no less effectively since then.)

Until the 1960's, white American culture publicly minimized the plight of the other two races through our history. There is nary a mention of the systematic genocide of native Americans, a practice that persisted from Columbus to Custer, in mainstream (read: "written by whites") history books; not surprisingly, there is just as little mention of the horrors and dehumanizing abuses of slavery. For most white Americans, the predominant historical image of the interaction between whites and Indians is that of benign "great white fathers" attempting to reach out to and civilize hostile native savages, with various degrees of success. The genocidal "resettlement" (not coincidentally, the same term used by the Nazis for the process of transporting Jews to concentration camps) which moved Indians from their native habitats to barren territories like Oklahoma is referred to in the history books written by whites with benign terms that might lead a naive reader to believe the resettlement process was a largely cooperative process, intended to be mutually beneficial to both races. Nowhere is the violation to the Indians or the extensive damage committed with callous disregard to their culture mentioned.

Similarly, the existence of Indian civilizations which were in many respects superior to those of the arriving European invaders, or the complete annihilation of such cultures by these invaders, are never mentioned. The images of slavery that pervade the consciousness of white Americans also come from white apologists, and from propagandist literature like *Gone With the Wind*. Such writings present a picture of benevolent white masters caring for and supporting otherwise ignorant and dependent slaves, rather than the more realistic view of slaves treated like so much livestock, with no rights of self-determination, no recourse against systematic abuses, and no acknowledgment that these exploited beings were human. In fact, the Constitution originally assigned to black slaves the status of three-fifths of a human being!

Mainstream American history books conveniently fail to mention that most of the signers of the Declaration of Independence, the document which forms the ideological foundation supporting the waging of the American Revolution, were slaveowners. They also ignore the central role of race in the westward expansion of the American nation, according to the doctrine of Manifest Destiny. One prominent example of such a convenient omission: even most college history majors are not aware that Texas' war of independence from Mexico was not fought to open up Texas for Anglo settlers, because such settlers were already freely allowed into the sparsely populated territory of "Tejas" by the ruling Mexican government. The war was fought to separate Texas from Mexican rule in order to open it to slavery, which was specifically prohibited by the recently established independent Mexican government. Awareness of this frequently and conveniently omitted historical fact puts the "heroic martyrs for freedom" at the Alamo in a whole new historical perspective, doesn't it? Upon the establishment of an Anglo government in Texas, one of the first acts of the new legislature was to expel free black persons from the new republic!

Consider these other influences and effects of slavery on some other important events in American history:

Few history students ever learn that the Mormons were driven out of Missouri, and subsequently took refuge in Utah, primarily because of their opposition to slavery. The War of 1812, which resulted in the burning of Washington, D.C. and the destruction of the White House, was initiated by white slave owners' desire to annex adjacent territory from Indian tribes, which were sympathetic towards and provided refuge to runaway slaves. The same is true of the Seminole Wars in Florida, the costliest Indian wars in American history, occurring between 1835 and 1842: President Andrew Jackson was not so covetous of acquiring territory in Florida, as he was desirous of destroying the Seminole tribe, which assimilated large numbers of runaway slaves from the nearby plantations of Georgia and Alabama. What's more, the Seminole tribe was not an Indian tribe, per se; it was a separate faction composed of people descended from intermarriages of Creek Indians and runaway African slaves, which may further explain the Seminoles' willingness to assimilate escaped slaves in large numbers. The role of race in these and other major historic events has been largely ignored or glossed over in the accounts written by establishment historians.

The same tendency to accept convenient myths, while excluding distasteful historical facts, is true of mainstream historians' treatment of many central figures in American history. Schoolchildren routinely learn of George Washington's unwillingness to lie to his father about chopping down the cherry tree, even though historians freely admit that this story has no basis in fact. Far fewer students of history learn that George Washington, "the father of our country," was a slave owner; that 87 percent of his administration's budget was devoted to military activity against Indian tribes; or that as President, he authorized the loan of hundreds of thousands of dollars to French plantation owners in Haiti, in order to aid these owners in suppressing a revolt by African slaves. This happened in the wake of his own nation's successful overthrow of British rule, an insurrection supposedly inspired by the spirit of freedom for all men. Washington did finally recognize the contradiction between his ownership of slaves and the stated ideals of the American Revolution, and at last freed his slaves—posthumously, in his will.

Patrick Henry, remembered by history books primarily for his declaration "give me liberty, or give me death!" in support of the American Revolution, was also a slave owner. Unable to reconcile the contradiction between his own stated inability to live without liberty and his apparent lack of concern or urgency in providing it for the hundreds of human beings he owned, Henry finally admitted, "I will not, I cannot justify it." But this inability to justify their bondage did not lead Mr. Henry to the presumed logical next step, the freeing of his slaves. Patrick Henry, like many of his contemporaries, chose to live with the dissonance of procuring freedom for white males like himself, while denying the same rights to human beings of other races, whose labors he shamelessly exploited.

The man behind the Declaration of Independence, the author of the key phrase "all men are created equal" which served as a central point in Martin Luther King's famous "I have a dream..." speech almost two centuries later, was also an unrepentant slave owner whose personal life contradicted the ideals he publicly promoted. Thomas Jefferson owned several hundred slaves over his lifetime, and grew fabulously wealthy through the exploitation of their labors on his behalf. Many decades before Franklin Roosevelt, Dwight Eisenhower, John Kennedy and Bill Clinton allegedly combined infidelity and sexual misadventures with the more straightforward duties of the Oval Office, Jefferson kept several favored female slaves as mistresses, and fathered a number of children with them. Like

Washington before him, when elected President, Jefferson actively supported the French plantation owners in Haiti in their struggle against the frequent revolts of their slaves, and advocated the expansion of slavery westward as the United States stretched its territories in that direction. When the Haitian slaves finally overthrew their owners and established a republic, the Jefferson administration denied the new nation diplomatic recognition, for fear that to do so would be tantamount to encouraging uprisings by slaves in the United States.

The liberation of Haiti from French rule ended Napoleon's ambitions for imperial expansion in the Americas, and led to the Louisiana Purchase, as Napoleon's priority was to finance his European military campaigns instead. No scholastic history books that I have encountered below the college level mention that the Louisiana Purchase simply bought out any French *claims* to the territory in question. France did not actually control these lands, which were occupied by a number of Indian tribes. However, it was just not an option, given the American government's mentality towards non-white people at that time, to consider negotiating with the Indian tribes which actually lived on these lands over territorial rights. Negotiation between "civilized" whites and non-white "savages" was unthinkable, because of the assumed disparity in relative development and sophistication between the races. Instead, the Jefferson administration simply bought the goodwill of Napoleon in purchasing the right to expand within lands simply *claimed* by France, and proceeded with the intention of simply brushing the native peoples aside, as needed. After all, United States policy towards Indian tribes occupying desired territory was already established by the time of Jefferson's presidency: Indians would be relocated or killed en masse in order to make way for the superior white invaders, without requiring their consent, or recognizing any perceived need to compensate them in any way.

Finally, Jefferson was the central figure behind the creation of the Democratic Party, which in the nineteenth century represented the interests of white supremacists and slave owners. This platform accounts for the popular support and dominance enjoyed by the Democratic party in Southern politics from Jefferson's time until the 1960's. By the middle of the 20th century, Democrats and Republicans were engaged in the process of reversing roles, with the former embracing civil rights and the latter becoming the party of the traditional establishment and the white conservatives. It is this role reversal between the parties that explains the emergence of Republican political dominance in the South over the last three decades, and renders some modern Republican politicians' claims to be perpetuating the traditions of "the party of Lincoln" ludicrous, since there are obvious fundamental contradictions between the policies of the populist and abolitionist Republican party of Lincoln's time, and Republican policies and initiatives in our own era. Such attempted comparisons sound particularly absurd when contrasted with the disgraceful civil rights record of modern Republicans like Strom Thurmond, Jesse Helms, Pat Buchanan and Ronald Reagan.

Even the earliest political hero of the civil rights movement, the author of the Emancipation Proclamation, does not come through with an image free of the racism that stains our history throughout. Abraham Lincoln stated plainly and emphatically during the Lincoln-Douglas debates that he was not in favor of bringing about the "social and political equality of the white and black races." Later, during the Civil War, he wrote to Horace Greeley at the *New York Tribune* that his priority as President was the preservation of the Union, and he was committed primarily to accomplishing this priority, whether doing so meant freeing the slaves or continuing slavery as it had existed. Yet Lincoln did transcend his own racism to respond to his emerging beliefs of moral certitude about the issue of slavery, which had divided his nation; he issued his Emancipation Proclamation just before the 1862 elections, fully aware that this would cost his party control of Congress, because the North had not yet embraced the anti-slavery sentiment which became more pervasive during the latter years of the Civil War.

Closer to our times, there are myriad examples of the effects of racism down through our history:

The U. S. Supreme Court upheld segregation in the landmark *Plessy v. Ferguson* case, as late as 1896, more than thirty years after Appomattox.

President Woodrow Wilson, a Jeffersonian Democrat and virulent southern racist, ran for the Presidency on a platform advocating civil rights. Once in office, one of his first acts was to formally order a policy of segregation within the federal government. When black federal workers protested, Wilson summarily fired them; when a delegation of prominent black community leaders came to implore him to reconsider, he dismissed them from the White House.

Wilson's formal establishment of racial inequality and separatism as official government policy was not an isolated historical manifestation of racism at the highest level of government. Following Wilson into the Oval Office, Warren G. Harding became the first American president—and hopefully the last!—to be formally inducted into the Ku Klux Klan during an official ceremony at the White House!

Racism actually increased in the period after the Civil War and Reconstruction, and was hardly confined to the South. Quality education for blacks during this period was simply unavailable. (Unfortunately, this condition has not substantially improved in our own time.) During Reconstruction, a great many idealistic young northerners went into the South to teach the freed slaves to read and write; most were subject to terrorist attacks, and several were murdered. It was in the aftermath of Reconstruction that American racist policy reached its nadir.

Following the Civil War, military expenditures were focused on westward expansion and the virtual elimination of the Indians from lands which were either agriculturally attractive, or had mineral deposits which white settlers coveted. This led to the massive "resettlement" and genocide that was directly responsible for the deaths of hundreds of thousands of Indians, and the relocation of others into areas so barren as to guarantee their perpetual impoverishment. Only a few decades later, Adolf Hitler frequently expressed admiration for the efficiency with which white America had herded native Americans into concentrated areas and restricted their numbers, in conversations with his intimate associates. In fact, Hitler modeled the Nazis' network of death camps designed specifically for the genocidal elimination of Jews, gypsies and other "undesirables" after the American "resettlement" of the Indians.

During this same post-Civil War period, racist suppression and persecution of blacks reached such depths throughout the country that might seem unbelievable to many among us today. Inadequate or nonexistent education, restricted access to the political process and to voting rights for Negroes, and violence in the form of lynchings and riots by whites became commonplace. African-Americans were routinely excluded from professional training programs, positions in civil service, and higher education; successful and socially prominent blacks were targeted for violence. The image of non-whites as sub-human flourished in the late nineteenth century in the United States, and American treatment of blacks and Indians became the model for South African *apartheid*, as well as for the official policies of segregation later instituted in Bermuda. The Bronx Zoo in New York actually exhibited a Negro man in a cage at the turn of the century!

Minstrel shows featuring whites acting as incompetent and bumbling Negroes were very popular, and these derogatory images endured in American theater and moviemaking from the late 19th century until well after World War II. The first motion picture with sound, a lengthy Hollywood "epic" titled *Birth of a Nation*, is also notable as one of the most virulent, blatantly racist works in any form of artistic expression. The comedies of the Marx Brothers, Laurel and Hardy, W.C. Fields, and the Three Stooges, and radio programs such as *Amos 'n Andy* (perhaps the most popular radio program in the history of American broadcasting), are replete with such degrading images of black people.

Well until after World War II, blacks could not buy houses in certain communities, could not get into trade unions, could not get into most colleges, could not work at jobs with high public visibility, like store salesmen and grocery clerks. Tragically, in many American communities and institutions these restrictions persist to this day, the sacrifices and struggles of people like Rosa Parks, Dr. King, and James Meredith notwithstanding. Blacks continue to be severely underrepresented in our time in the graduate schools, board rooms and places of power within our culture.

There is a dearth of educational opportunity that is responsible for this deprivation and inequality, as well as a subtle but insidious conditioning that channels minority children away from opportunities in education, to which a far greater number can have access, encouraging them instead towards athletics and entertainment, where the opportunities are far more limited. Seduced by the public exposure given to black multimillionaires like Michael Jordan, Whitney Houston, Ken Griffey Jr., and Michael Jackson, black youths aspire to the very limited opportunity to emulate them. Far fewer aspire to become the next Thurgood Marshall, Faye Wattleton, Alan Page or Alex Haley—not surprising in a culture which gives only passing and grudging acknowledgment to black intellectual accomplishments. In turning away from academics, black children are undoubtedly influenced by a society that projects very low expectations on them in this area. The most disturbing recent example of white disparagement and discouragement of black intellectual development was the recent publication of the pseudoscientific and ultra-racist book, *The Bell Curve*, which employs very questionable methods and reasoning in attempting to "scientifically" confirm the inherent intellectual inferiority of blacks, in comparison to whites.

The enduring tragedy of American society is that there has been a succession of ethnic groups arriving on our shores, and struggling against decades of resistance, hostility, and violence to be assimilated into the mainstream. Once each of these groups has gained assimilation into the social mainstream, it has failed to learn from the experiences of its struggle to be included in the social fabric. Each of them has, virtually without exception, then turned around and continued the socially abusive cycle by resisting the assimilation of subsequent groups in the same manner that they had to overcome and transcend. It may be the nature of human beings to avoid learning from their own life experiences, and thus being condemned to repeating the history they have resisted learning. Whatever the case, there can be little doubt that the American "melting pot" is a myth; American society is composed of a series of strata, in which prejudice and discrimination flow downward, and in which clannish exclusionism uneasily coexists with some unavoidable ethnic blending.

Sociopolitical commentator John Leo, writing in his column in *U. S. News and World Report*, effectively illustrated the effects of prejudice and bias in creating destructive and abusive, but totally unnecessary, perceptions in our society—as well as the irrationality of this perspective. Mr. Leo recently wrote about an ethnic group that came to the United States under duress, in great numbers, and was immediately shunted to the bottom of the societal pecking order. This group was disturbingly over-represented in the prison population, in statistics about crime and violence, and in unemployment. It was grossly *under*represented in the work force, in the schools, and among professional, "white collar" occupations. Social commentators frequently expressed despair about this ethnic group's disproportionate contribution to the formation of a permanent underclass, to unemployment and crime statistics, and to the perceived high probability of its perpetually requiring a substantial portion of public funds in order to sustain even minimally acceptable levels of existence. Many of these same commentators voiced their theories, which postulated the possibility that members of this nationality suffered from genetic deficiencies which would render them forever inferior and subordinate in American society. The ethnic group referred to by Mr. Leo was the Irish, and the observations and commentary about them were drawn from writings of the mid-19th century. It was Mr. Leo's point, of course, to compare these perceptions and reactions about the Irish more than a century ago to those aimed towards African-Americans in our own time. I was struck by the similarity of these remarks about the two groups, which clearly indicate how little progress we have made in our collective consciousness over the last century in ethnic and racial relations. All we seem able to do is shift our focus from one group to another.

Of course, the Irish are no longer subject to such social perceptions. They have risen to the highest levels of society, and have been represented at the highest levels of government, professional circles and culture. Like the Irish, other European and Asian nationalities have taken their turn on the bottom rung of the social chain, and endured prejudice, abuse and violence. Stereotypes about various groups endure, with varying proportions of humor and malice included in the use of these stereotypic images, depending on the group's level of assimilation within the mainstream of our society. According to some of the more common of these stereotyped images, Irish tend to be alcoholics, Italians participate in or at least support organized crime, Hispanics tend to be overly emotional and temperamental, Jews are good businessmen and "tight" with money, Orientals are good with mathematics, Germans are cold and cruel, Blacks are lazy, French are pompous and clannish, Scots are very frugal, and so on. Whatever the basis for such stereotypes, they do more to separate us and encourage conflict between us than they contribute to our understanding of one another, or to a unified society.

In many respects, we have made significant progress in race relations since the civil rights movement of the 1960's. However, in many areas discrimination keeps many of our citizens deprived and oppressed by unequal opportunity and unequal access to education and earning ability. The apparent contradiction between these two statements can be best understood if one comes to realize that in some areas of American life racism and its effects have been virtually eliminated, but in other respects racism has merely become more subtle and covert, but no less virulent or influential.

Formal racial discrimination has nearly disappeared from most public areas of American life, but continues virtually unabated and unchanged within some communities and social organizations. Race is second only to gender in determining whom most Americans will choose as a mate, and remains an important factor in employment practices, church and club membership, and choice of residential location. It is a significant factor in political races, in some cases by influencing the sympathies of the electorate, and in others by determining the viability of potential candidates. Perceptions of racial (in)sensitivity have both won and lost political races, as the recent campaigns of Pat Buchanan and Jesse Helms have illustrated, also showing that racial insensitivity can be both a political asset and a liability, depending on the inclinations of the electorate. More disturbing is the recent example of General Colin Powell's potential presidential candidacy, announced before the 1996 election. General Powell was considered by far the most attractive of the potential aspirants for the Republican nomination by many analysts before the primaries, but unexpectedly withdrew from consideration. One of the reasons he gave for his withdrawal was his family's concern for his safety, because they recognized that the racial climate across much of the nation was not yet prepared to accept an African-American President, and that there was a strong possibility that he might be assassinated if there appeared to be a high probability of his election. We have a long way to go in eliminating the effects of racism and violence from our political process, and this is one of the important factors which render descriptions of the United States as a "democracy" sadly preposterous.

Race is still a significant, and for minorities a very limiting, factor in hiring practices and economic opportunity. Unemployment for minority groups is significantly higher than the overall statistic. Under-employment statistics are not kept because of the difficulty in defining underemployed status in individual cases; but there is reason to believe that, with significant overall unemployment among ethnic minorities, those who do manage to find paying positions often have to settle for less demanding and less economically attractive jobs.

There is much to be said against the practices of zoning both in real estate and for political purposes, as well. In real estate, minorities are typically shunted to designated areas, so as not to allow intermixing of whites with minorities. One of the more outrageous American traditions is the effect of race on real estate values, which prevents minority buyers with the economic ability to move into some affluent predominantly white neighborhoods from actually doing so, and which drastically but artificially lowers the area's prices when a minority person does gain residence in the area. Similarly, areas and boundaries for political voting districts are often manipulated and distorted so as to contain, isolate and minimize the voting influence of minority ethnic groups. In practice, racial relations in America emphasize separatism without much equality, except on the most superficial levels.

Racism still influences other significant areas of our society, and deprivation of economic opportunity for minorities is responsible for many of these racially-determined disparities. Like it or not, economic deprivation is strongly correlated to lower IQ scores, diminished quality of education, substandard nutrition, lower life expectancy, higher crime rates, and all the other factors considered in determining a person's quality of life. Thus, there continues to manifest a disturbing disparity among the races in our society, and the prevailing social trend seems to inspire greater pessimism for our future, if polls among our young are to be believed. Recent nationwide polls among high school students of all races indicate that a very pessimistic view about the future of race relations in America is increasingly prevalent among our young people.

One of the necessary prerequisites to the improvement of the dreary state of race relations in America is the acknowledgment and teaching in our schools of the heritage of discrimination and racial abuse in our past. To the extent that we ignore the abuses and injustices of our ancestors, we are condemned to repeat them, as we have already learned by our collective resistance to assimilating new immigrant groups. Integration and blending of the races is also essential as a policy in all our institutions, because fear and prejudice are most effectively cultivated from a distance. Once we come to appreciate each other as human beings, we can begin to accept the individual traits that attract us to one another; until then, the separation created by the perception of "us" and "them" along racial lines will increase the separation and fear between us, and continue to hamper and trivialize our collective achievements.

Chapter 3

Work and Vocations

Choosing one's work and purpose in life should be a very simple process. Each of us is born with certain talents, which become apparent fairly early in life. They fit us like an old pair of jeans, and we enjoy doing the activities involved with them so much, they hardly feel like work at all. Unfortunately, a series of influences often interferes and diverts us from our life's purpose, directing us towards the pursuit of studies and careers that have nothing to do with our true calling in life. Once again, the preconceptions of parents, teachers, friends and other well-meaning people intrude, and redirect our efforts towards pursuits that may be rated highly in terms of the social status, earning power, or prestige they afford, without adequately considering the enjoyment or genuine satisfaction these may hold for that person. Far too many people are driven by the perceived need to satisfy parental expectations and social

demands, and forget in the process that they will be performing
the tasks of their vocation for most of their adult life, and would
therefore be well advised to choose some activity that they enjoy
and will look forward to performing.

In my practice and daily life, I have encountered a number
of people who have trained in a particular vocation in order to
meet some expectations imposed on them by others, or because
of an abstract assumption that they owe it to themselves to
attain a certain professional status or income level that they
can't imagine achieving in any other way. Indeed, for many of
them, their career choice becomes more than that—it becomes
their identity, and in the process they forget the actual person
underneath that label or public persona, as well as that person's
emotional tendencies and needs. They become "Dr. _____,"
"_____, Attorney at Law," "The Most Rev. ____," or take on
one of a variety of other labels, at the expense of their person-
hood. The greatest problem, of course, is that it's very difficult
to have a personal relationship with an impersonal role. So
many people go through life with a variety of associates,
colleagues and business acquaintances, but with a dearth of
real friends and lovers that they are all too often oblivious to
until much later in life. When the time comes to reassess their
existence, they have a series of accomplishments, honors,
awards and successful financial deals to point out, but it may
be only at this late stage of their life that they may come to
realize how desperately alone and lonely they have been, and

how little *personal* satisfaction can be derived through honors, awards and fat bank accounts. In John Bradshaw's words, such people have forgotten that they are human beings, and have become "human doings," people who define their value and self-worth by their accomplishments and achievements, rather than an intrinsic awareness of the divine and absolute essence of all humans.

Allow me to illustrate the point with a few anecdotes from my personal experiences. I've had the good fortune to have as a professional mentor a man who was a wealthy farmer early in life, one who benefitted from government contracts to build for himself and his family an annual income well in excess of a million dollars per year, while he was still in his 20's! He had money beyond his wildest dreams, ample leisure time, and as secure a financial future as he could imagine. He also had a very unhappy marriage and a vocation that didn't utilize his intelligence and talents anywhere near their fullest capacity. His life bored him to tears.

This man was restricted in his life choices by a strong sense of obligation to a family that provided him with little emotional gratification, and tormented him with constant reminders of their demands and expectations regarding his capacity to continue supporting them financially in a lifestyle to which they had already become accustomed. In short, he was confined to a very unsatisfying lifestyle with no relief in sight, and with his own sense of obligation to his family and feelings of guilt cementing his plight. As he once observed, it's no wonder they call material goods "the *trappings* of wealth;" he felt trapped in his situation as securely as he would have been in any maximum-security prison.

My future mentor spent most of his days at the country club, playing golf and cards between drinking bouts with "buddies" who shared his economic wealth, plentiful leisure time and emotional poverty. He was there to escape from the stress and deprivation in his home life, as were most of his cronies. He drank very heavily, smoked at least two packs of cigarettes a day, and rarely spent time with his family. In the process, he developed heart disease at a level serious enough to warrant several lengthy hospitalizations, which he attributed to his smoking and stress; how appropriate an ailment for someone with so little love and nurturing in his life! Most people perceived him as being considerably older than his near-thirty years. In short, he was using his activities and chemical addictions to numb himself from his distress, and escape from his family situation in the only ways that were acceptable to him and his social circle, even if that meant the deterioration of his health and his slow but certain self-destruction. By his own account, given his religious beliefs, he would have rather died than divorced. Changing vocations was also utterly unthinkable, since it would mean dramatically lowering his family's financial status.

Deliverance came to this man suddenly and unexpectedly: the spouse he could not stand living with, but could not bear to divorce because of his family's religious and moral beliefs, suddenly fell ill and died. Her death freed him to leave his property and most of his financial holdings to his children, with whom he shared no close emotional bonds, and to return to school. He earned a doctorate in counseling by his late 30's, accepted a teaching post at a rural southwestern college, and remarried. He is currently earning a comfortable salary, but one that is less than one-thirtieth of what he used to earn as a farmer, and he is happier than he could have ever imagined being "in that other life" he once led. Not coincidentally, he now looks far younger than his numerical age. He makes it a point to never work more than six hours a day, and to use his leisure time to enjoy himself. He quit smoking many years ago, and will only rarely indulge in an occasional "social drink." He also boasts in private that his new bride, several years his junior, can hardly keep up with him in the bedroom. If you saw him, you would understand the real, profound meaning of "born again."

When I was in graduate school, working towards my degree in psychology, I maintained some close friendships with several people who were students in law school. During our social gatherings away from the books, I would notice that we took a very different approach towards our studies, and therefore allowed them to influence our overall lifestyle very differently as well. Graduate students in the liberal arts, like psychology, studied in an environment that promoted and rewarded originality and creativity; they worked under relatively little pressure and performance anxiety, since the typical grade range was from A to A- or B. In most cases, there were no required class examinations, with a term paper or project used to determine class grades. Class discussions took place in casual, seminar-style groups, somewhat resembling the repartee on television discussion programs. Often, preliminary work on projects and papers was done in groups, and wine or beer were often served during and after these gatherings.

By contrast, my friends in law school found themselves in a competitive, adversarial situation, where long hours of study and memorization were the norm, and close adherence to the textbook contents was required. Grades were given in rank order of the class, so that one's classmates were one's most immediate competitors, as well. When I would visit the law school in the period just before final exams, the very perceptible tension in the air "could be cut with a knife." After graduation, similar patterns were observed: Liberal arts students went into business for themselves, or acquired jobs with various universities, agencies and organizations. Fledgling lawyers competed with each other for positions in prestigious law firms, and the ones with the dubious good fortune of landing the more desirable jobs received handsome salaries—which were compensation for work schedules that frequently reached or exceeded 80 hours a week, with little room for a personal life. When any of my lawyer friends mentioned that they were in the process of preparing for a case to be presented in court, that was an indirect way of announcing that it would be fruitless to attempt any social contact with them until further notice.

Please understand: This is not an argument specifically against turning to the law as a course of study; but it *is* an argument for avoiding high-stress, low-satisfaction careers that entice one with high pay and status, when such a choice might yield a lifestyle filled with pressure, stress and little opportunity for nurturing oneself and personal growth. The law isn't the only area where such high-stress careers might be found; I merely used it as an example because of my familiarity with it. The advertising industry, the financial sector, and any number of high-volume corporations use monetary rewards to entice potential employees into career paths that promise great financial gains, but frequently combine these gains with low life satisfaction and limited personal development. The increasing complexity of society spawns such career options almost on a daily basis, and the insecure but gifted among us are easily seduced by the "tender trap" of monetary reward and financial security at the expense of their humanity. Indeed, many people in such positions have been overheard referring to their career as the "golden handcuffs" that bind them to an unsatisfying and even self-destructive lifestyle. Often, their ultimate reward is an early heart attack, a bout with cancer, multiple chemical addictions, and recurring divorces. Go stand on one of the main streets in any major city, at a time when most employees are commuting to their jobs. As they walk from their cars or from public transportation to their office buildings, notice their eyes and facial expressions: far too many of their faces are drawn and devoid of any sign of joy, of any enthusiasm for life, looking as if they're on strong sedatives; their eyes stare straight ahead, blank and unfocused, without any of the sparkle of a person whose life is "on purpose." From mail-room clerks to highly-paid executives, they go daily "once more into the breach" in order to maintain their lifestyle or just their temporary survival, with little emotion or love attached to their task. Their company buys their acquiescence, allegiance and continued adherence to the system by providing them with their remuneration, while securing multiple profits based on their efforts.

As an added inducement, there is the "carrot" of health insurance and retirement plans dangled before them. These programs are often more limited than their intended benefits, due to cutbacks, changes in coverage, or cited "pre-existing conditions." With increasing frequency, workers are simply terminated before their access to such "security" can begin, as a cost-cutting measure to both employers and insurance companies. Yet the illusion of "security," along with the dubious reassurance of a recurring paycheck, keeps so many people from realizing their life's dreams and benefitting themselves from the full range of their abilities.

This continued mass hypnosis, promoted by an educational system founded on the myth of "to get a good job, get a good education," has continued to lure the insecure into career paths promising comfort and security, while delivering sustenance and exploitation. The myth offered by organized religion of a reward in the afterlife in return for subservience and sacrifice in this life has been somewhat modified by corporate society, to a promise for financial security in retirement in return for loyalty and adherence to an economic system which is meant to benefit the powerful elite through most of a person's productive years. There are still too few people like Jason Robards' character, Murray, in the movie *A Thousand Clowns*, who are willing to turn their back on the system that has fundamentally failed them, and reconstruct their lives along more sensible, if less conventional, parameters. Instead, more than one hundred years after the Emancipation Proclamation, there are so many who allow their insecurities and fears about the future to lure them into voluntary servitude from which they will not emerge until the twilight of their life—if at all.

There are encouraging signs of an approaching transformation in philosophy in this area, an undercurrent of change which promises to unleash a new wave of independence and creativity that will permanently alter the current business and career establishment for the better, in spite of itself. If government statistics are a faithful indicator, more and more people of all ages, educational levels and ethnic groups are now looking towards self-employment as the direction of their lives. Tens of thousands of people no longer appear in employment or *non*employment statistics. Many of these new entrepreneurs fail in their first (and second) attempts, but struggle again and again to make it on their own. They are succeeding in record numbers, too, encouraging more and more others to follow them out of the corporate boardroom and into their own home or office. Such people are not confirmed pessimists, defeatists who have given up on ever securing a piece of the corporate pie; nor are they socialists, looking to fall back on the weak safety net of government services and the largesse of the wealthy in order to secure a meager survival. They are believers in the full range of their abilities, people who know that a belief in oneself is more valuable than any number of M.B.A.'s or Ph.D.'s in securing a healthy portion of the world's unlimited wealth for themselves. In the process, they have designed original and flexible work schedules that leave them time for relationships and a personal life, the pursuit of second careers or other interests, time with their children and spouses, and more "quality time" in their lives than ever before.

How does one go about freeing oneself to pursue a dream, and in the process provide oneself with enough material comforts to end all wants and needs? By starting from the end result you desire and working backwards. Each of us has a calling, a talent, a skill that we perform as well as or better than anyone else on earth. What's more, each of us feels most comfortable when performing this skill, so that it seems more play and recreation than work. Deepak Chopra calls this our "dharma," a Sanskrit word that roughly translates to one's "purpose in life." When you're in "dharma," you know it, as surely as you know it when you're in the right relationship, or when you have made the right decision. Like being in love, there is no mistaking it when it is there! When everyone in the world is in "dharma," there will be such peace, creativity and sheer bliss in the world as to make it indeed a "heaven on earth."

Decide what you would like to do if you already had all the money in the world that you could ever possibly need. If you were already "there" financially, what would you occupy yourself with to give your life purpose and to benefit your fellow man, as well? (Okay, what would you do *after* you bought all the cars, boats and houses, and went on all the trips and vacations you wanted to go on?) Some might choose to work with the mentally ill, others with the homeless, others might counsel inner-city youth, still others might provide low-cost services to depressed areas, or pro bono legal care, or work within educational systems. You get the idea; these are only a few possibilities, and not one one-thousandth of one percent of all the essential services needed by humanity. Wherever you feel called, and are comfortable, there your bliss and your satisfaction lie, and there you will also find your "horn of plenty" with regard to material wealth. The wealth will come to you as effortlessly as the work you do comes through you. It is absolutely not true that the world of business has to be a dog-eat-dog arena, where the fit survive by consuming the weak; that is simply the experience of many among us, consistent with their expectations of the situation.

There's ample wealth to go around for everyone, and you can most easily realize it by realizing your purpose and helping your fellow man. So, if you're not there yet, go design your better and more desirable career, and start *now* towards realizing it—even if it means slowly saving towards it and completing some preliminary plans, so your current job can become far more palatable by becoming transformed into a means towards a better end. Comfort and life satisfaction are not the province of a privileged few, but the birthright of all of us. If that's not your current life condition, it's because you are, however subconsciously, holding yourself away from your heart's desires. As soon as you reverse this trend, as soon as you get out of your own way and start working in conjunction with your desires, the world's bounty will unfold itself before your feet. Start allowing it to do so now! Remember, it has nothing to do with whether you deserve it or not; there is no doubt that you do. It's your birthright, and your natural place in Creation.

Chapter 4

Relationships

In an age where the search for fulfillment in life and spiritual awareness are slowly but surely replacing the mindless search for definition and glorification of the individual, relationships and the sense of connection among us seem more essential than ever. The sense of alienation and diminished value of the individual seems to be more widespread, with more and more people feeling unsatisfied and empty in the pursuits and tasks of their daily lives, and increasingly lost and devalued as individuals. Feeling like just another number, whether it be the number of your social security card, bank account or credit card, is a very common feeling and frequently voiced source of dissatisfaction with life. Yet, at the time when we seem in greatest need of discovering the deep meaning of our existence in the most profound manner possible—our sense of connection to each other—a good number of us are experiencing a period of separation and alienation unparalleled in history.

In many ways, our separateness and loneliness seem to be the defining malaise of our age. (This is hardly surprising, one would suppose, after two decades of emphasis on materialism and the "me" generation.) Even more discouraging are reports about spiraling divorce rates and the dissolution of the extended family as a functional entity. Moreover, our ever-growing communities and overcrowded cities have brought greater numbers of people within very close physical proximity, while we ironically have almost simultaneously lost the sense of community and mutual reliance that bound other societies together in the past. Some of our alienation has to do with developments in our technology that make it easy to entertain ourselves and "commune" with one another through television and computers, at the expense of a more personal connection.

Functions that increased one's sense of community and mutual reliance have disappeared, or been severely altered. Bartering of services, for example: fixing of a neighbor's leaky roof in return for a home-baked pie or home-cooked dinner, has been replaced by reliance on professional workmen and restaurants. Meeting friends and the courting process, once done within community activities or church groups, have now moved to the business board room, the health club, and bars and clubs catering to the seekers of companionship. Professional dating services and activity organizers now abound, overtaking common functions formerly handled informally among friends; their advertisements can be easily found in most magazines and newspapers. In the process, personal connections and the cultivation of social skills suffer. But perhaps the greatest tragedy is that we have lost the sense of one another—and, by extension, ourselves—because we have become so busy and specialized that we have reduced human beings to their most basic functions, forgetting the inner person that lies under it all. We use answering and fax machines to leave messages; we may choose to send pre-printed cards and gifts that a service chooses for us. We get together with and fall apart from our mates because of tax advantages, pre-nuptual agreements, community settlements, separation of property, and social implications. We have sets of friends that we alternately have drinks with, go double-dating with, ask professional advice from, have sex with, escort to important occasions, play tennis or golf with, and use to get away from our mates, family or other friends. In short, we have relationships with a series of roles and functions, not with complete other persons. Very few of us can be said to have relationships any more; instead, most of us have a series of mutually agreed-upon arrangements with a variety of persons, who are defined far more clearly by their function and role(s) in our lives than by any quality that makes them unique or special to us in and of themselves. Of course, since our relationships tend to mirror our awareness and our mindset, that also means that most of us have defined and limited ourselves by the roles we have assumed, as well; and in fact, for many people, the sudden deprivation of a label such as "mother," "teacher," "accountant" or "club member" would constitute a real identity crisis. Not being able to perceive ourselves as more than a collection of roles and functions, we are only able to give of ourselves within the limits of those roles and functions, and to receive in kind.

It seems ironic that, at a time when relationships and a sense of connections to others seem more important than ever and our ability to communicate and travel has "shrunk the world" to heretofore unimagined accessibility, the emotional distance between people seems so great. Perhaps a recent emphasis on the independence of the individual, along with a change in the perception of the likelihood or probability of permanence in relationships, have contributed to many contemporary relationships becoming more limited and more superficial in nature. Perhaps the greater focus on dysfunctional families and collective pathology emphasized by recent trends in psychotherapy have altered people's perceptions, and increased pessimism about the possibility of truly nurturing and mutually supportive connections occurring among two people. Whatever the reasons, it is clear that for most of us, it is becoming more and more difficult to escape the trap of mistrust, cynicism and alienation that have so effectively separated us from most of our fellow human beings.

Why are relationships so difficult? A great many things can go wrong in a relationship, for a variety of reasons. Research and greater knowledge about family systems and interpersonal dynamics have led to a greater understanding of the complex contributing factors that go into personality development, and influence the ways in which we relate to others. Perhaps the most significant of these is the person's experience in the family of origin, a commonly held view that seems to have a lot of validity. This view holds that the ways in which we were trained to relate to our parents, and the issues that were significant during our childhood, will emerge in our adult relationships, both complicating them and inviting resolution. While it is not the purpose of this work to examine such dynamics in detail, it would be useful for the reader who has experienced recurring difficulties in interpersonal relationships to refer to the works of pioneering counselors and scholars in this area. However, this is not to be perceived as an acceptable substitute for some honest self-examination with the assistance of a skilled therapist. For anyone having an interest in this area, I particularly recommend the writings of Harville Hendrix, Virginia Satir, Patricia Love, Jay Haley, Beverly DeAngelis and R. D. Laing.

Assuming that you have had the normally allotted episodes and adventures in relationships, you will have undoubtedly found that a series of attempts to form intimacy bonds with a number of apparently dissimilar people has resulted in similarly dissatisfying results. Moreover, you're likely to observe, with only mild introspection, that the reasons for the ultimate dissolution of your relationships are remarkably consistent in relationship after relationship, in spite of an array of apparently disparate personalities among your lovers—again, this is no coincidence. Alas, until we gain further insight, we are all very likely to purchase the same book over and over again, deceived by a different cover. There is an even more disturbing insight there: in most cases, we are likely to *create* the same book under dissimilar-looking covers! How can that be, and why would any rational-thinking person—such as you!—possibly want to keep getting into, and even creating, such unpleasant situations? Well, for a variety of reasons, the simplest of which are that a) the choice is not made on a conscious level, and b) we keep returning to the issues that cause distress in our lives until we resolve them (and the arena of interpersonal relationships is our most pressing area!) So, armed with that knowledge, you will now be even more motivated to resolve your relationship issues, knowing that your alternatives otherwise are to either continue to have dissatisfying relationships, or to remain alone. Some people *do* actually choose one of these two; you may even know someone who has done so, but if happiness, self-awareness and spiritual fulfillment are your goals, I wouldn't recommend either!

Okay, so how do you go about fixing your relationships? You're very likely not going to like this answer, either: you don't; you fix yourself! Why? Because you may, when you look over your past history in relationships, discover that not only were there some issues that remain constant, but that there was another constant in that equation. It was always *you*, plus another person that constituted the relationship. No matter how similar or different the people you were involved with were, you were always an essential part of the mix.

By some honest and open self-examination, you'll quickly arrive at the issues you have yet to resolve that keep getting between you and intimacy. This can be a useful learning experience on many levels, but is particularly useful on those infrequent opportunities when you get a second chance at a past relationship. It is a common human trait to look back on certain past relationships with longing, especially during times when you are feeling lonely, and to remember the good aspects of those experiences, while ignoring or conveniently forgetting the reasons why you're no longer in that relationship. We are all on certain life paths, with lessons to be learned in this incarnation; that is also true for those who come into, and then go out of our lives. They have their path to travel as well, with issues to be confronted and lessons to be learned; and chances are that they were working on those lessons when we met them the last time around, and will still be doing so when we meet them again.

It is a characteristic of human nature that, in times of loneliness, we tend to remember the good about those who have passed out of our life and whom we miss, and forget their more trying traits and qualities. So it is that sometimes we get a second chance with such a person, and a second opportunity to be reminded of the reasons we left the first time. I was once in a relationship with a woman with whom I was deeply infatuated, and with whom I seemed to have so much in common. We not only had a very exciting sexual relationship, but we enjoyed long conversations and common interests, similar activities, the same music, foods, etc. However, this woman had some very strong issues about abandonment of which I gradually became aware. When she became emotionally involved with someone, rather than risk losing them and experience the pain of abandonment again, she would drive them away with contrived accusations of various transgressions, accompanied by very intense displays of rage. I came to understand that the intensity of her rage was correlated to the intensity of her fear of experiencing the pain of loss and separation again. Indeed, after several months of a very rewarding relationship, these rage-filled episodes emerged more and more frequently. I felt powerless to resolve them or help her get past them, and decided to spare myself further emotional abuse by leaving the relationship. This was after I became frustrated with my repeated ineffectual efforts to "fix" our relationship, and make it and her "better." Six months later, she found an occasion to get back in touch with me again, and since I wasn't in another meaningful relationship at the time,

I allowed the memories of our passion and emotional closeness in the past to bring us together again.

Well, you probably can already guess what happened. Some time down the line, when once again I felt comfortable and deeply involved in the relationship, the episodes of rage began to occur with increasing frequency. This time, I was much quicker in deciphering the handwriting on the wall—I even recognized the penmanship! I left the relationship again, far more easily and quickly than the first time. As fate and this woman would have it, after a few months she contacted me a third time; but this time, remembering *all* of my former experiences with her, I tossed the letter away with a wistful smile, and didn't even respond to it. My thoughts on the matter were that I didn't need another turn on *that* emotional merry-go-round. I still remember that relationship as one of the most intense and deeply loving ones I ever had, and to this day I think of this woman with great fondness. However, I also remember the emotional cycle involved, and would never think of entering it yet again.

Our relationships are reflections of our self-image, which includes our expectations, as opposed to our aspirations, and some idea of what and whom we deserve to have in our lives. Since we always get what we expect and feel we deserve, it's important to have a very clear idea of whom we want in our life, and in what capacity. Because of their training and past experiences, many people who become aware of this natural law feel compelled to include some limitations of their "ideal" person, along with all of the positive qualities. They believe that, by imposing certain limits and flaws on the person they are trying to attract, that they will have a better chance of actually allowing *anyone at all* into their life. Their experiences and beliefs have convinced them that limits are a necessary part of reality, and no condition can "realistically" come into their life that does not include some limits as a requisite for being "real." Moreover, and of equal importance, they believe that such a person (with an "appropriate" array of flaws and limitations) will be someone they have a better chance of holding onto, because such a person would match their own perceived imperfections, and therefore be less likely to become disillusioned with them and reject them. Such people settle into life conditions that they perceive as "good enough," instead of reaching for the sky with their dreams and aspirations. The lesson here is to place no limits on your dreams and happiness; you can have as attractive and loving a person as you wish in your life, as well as health, wealth and comfort. Imposing limits on your life and your expectations is only another way of criticizing and withholding from yourself the luxury and bounty of the universe that is yours for the asking! You may think that you are protecting yourself from abandonment and rejection when you attempt to set "realistic" limits to your expectations; however, abandonment and rejection only occur when the right person or condition is not in your life, and they are simply ways of making room for that better situation to occur.

Don't be upset or linger over "time invested," and now lost, in a relationship. The time you put in was worth the time; you learned from the experience, grew, and can now move on. When someone or something you thought you wanted or needed leaves your life, send it/them away in love, and keep looking for your bliss! It's there, and it's yours for the asking!

Finally, don't settle for what you think you can have, as opposed to what you really want, in a relationship. There are no "perfect" people, and the capacity to be accepting of some idiosyncracies and differences is part of even the best relationships; but it is important to be honest with yourself and with your partner, and to not settle for relationships that don't meet your intimacy and nurturing needs, nor are likely to in the near future. Certainly, one should not exchange one partner for another with the frequency we change our underwear; that kind of superficial examination and exchange in personal relationships is very much a part of the malaise of our times—and indicative of the lack of depth so many in our time bring to personal commitments. However, if you have arrived at the painful awareness that your basic intimacy and commitment needs are not likely to be met in your current relationship, you owe it to yourself and to your partner to let go of one another in love, and resume the search. It's one of the unfortunate and common symptoms of our age that so many of us are afraid of all but the most superficial commitments, out of a persistent need to "avoid getting hurt." We don't recognize that using this excuse to continually choose loneliness and alienation is the *ultimate* pain! Very few people seem to realize that reaching a place of disagreement and conflict is normal in *all* relationships, and that in fact the resolution of these conflicts is what gives relationships substance and depth. Staying with and resolving those conflicts may frequently be difficult and painful, but the reward after resolution is a bond of such closeness and intimacy that makes the whole process well worth it.

If you're involved with a person whom you recognize as being emotionally unavailable, fearful of deep commitment and intimacy, or reliant on abuse and manipulation for control and emotional extortion, and who is not open to acknowledging or seeking help for these shortcomings, you owe it to yourself to leave and keep searching for a more satisfactory relationship. Some self-examination as to why you chose and were willing to settle for such an inadequate relationship in the first place wouldn't hurt, either, especially before you go on looking for the next one. Remaining in unhappy relationships opens the door for addictive and compulsive behaviors, overworking, and other forms of self-abuse. It gives your subconscious mind the message, "I'm not worth any better than this, and don't deserve higher expectations; therefore, I'm not worth taking good care of, even by myself." If this describes your situation, you owe it to both of you to make a move, and to do so without lingering or procrastinating. Drawing out the breakup process is not saving anyone from pain or hurt, and is in fact prolonging and intensifying the process. Once your mind is made up, inform your partner without malice or rancor, and go. Moreover, don't allow considerations such as shared property, finances, etc., to hold you back; when in doubt, leave it/them behind, and *go*! Material objects and money can be replaced; your life and emotional health cannot.

A particular word of advice to parents here: if you're staying in a dysfunctional or abusive relationship "for the sake of the children," you're not doing either the children or yourself any favors! People who use that excuse are, in reality, using their children as a noble-sounding excuse to cover up their reluctance to act in their own behalf. This is not noble, and hardly conducive to a better life for any of the persons involved. Growing up in an emotional "war zone" is never healthy for children, and in fact teaches them that they have an obligation to also linger in abusive and dysfunctional relationships when they reach adulthood.

It is not true that there is only one, perfect partner for everyone out there. However, it *is* true that there are several people out there in the world with whom you could have a very happy and satisfying coexistence. You owe it to yourself, and to them, to make the effort required to find one another. When you do, you'll know it! You'll not only improve your relationships and your capacity to meet your emotional needs, but every aspect of your life. That's because it all comes back to the fact that, in order to have a good relationship with another, we must have a good relationship with ourselves first. Once we're okay with us, we ask for and manifest only the best for us, in all areas of our life. It is then that life truly becomes worth living!

Chapter 5

Family Dynamics

The family is widely assumed to be the basic unit of a functional society. A substantial proportion of politicians, theologians, philosophers and psychotherapists consider the stability and survival of the traditional two-parent family unit as essential to a functional, morally sound and stable society. The decline of the proportion of traditional families in the overall population has been blamed by a wide cross-section of moralists, religious leaders and social scientists for everything from the proliferation of drug abuse and the spread of AIDS to the rise in teen sexual activity and decline in citizens' participation in churches and politics. Certainly, the perceptions and functions of the American family have undergone several significant transformations in the post-World War II era. However, no discussion of the changes affecting American families can be complete without a consideration of the changes and trends in the overall culture that influences and supports these transformations.

The decline in the occurrence and perceived desirability of the traditional family unit may be attributed to a variety of changes and trends in the last couple of generations. Some of the major influences to be considered in understanding this trend are: a) the changes and advances effected by the women's movement in redefining the functions and roles of women, as well as men, within society; b) the increasing disillusionment and cynicism with which traditional institutions, including the two-parent, heterosexual family, are perceived; c) the more widespread acceptance for alternative lifestyles and living arrangements; d) the social proliferation of an "instant gratification" mentality which includes tolerance for change, experimentation and short-term planning—all of which work against long-term stability, promote less rigidly defined individual roles, and intolerance towards rigid systems in any area of life.

The women's liberation movement, which hit its stride in America in the late 1960's and early 1970's, marked the widespread emergence of women's demands to be accepted as equal partners in personal relationships, as well as in the work force and within society in general. In personal relationships, this marked a departure from the traditional view of women as keepers of the household and supporters of their man as he pursued a career and financially supported the family. Many women were no longer content to be "the power behind the throne," or to confine their own career aspirations to child rearing and housekeeping. For some, the choice was made to forego traditional marriage entirely in the pursuit of professional careers, and/or motherhood without the inclusion or active participation of the biological father. In some cases, this meant a reversal of traditional roles, with the woman pursuing advanced education and assuming the responsibility of primary financial provider, while the man assumed child rearing and household duties. In other cases, a woman's family of origin, friends and professional support systems (such as a day-care center or school) all participated in caring for children while the woman pursued education and career. Many women chose to forego having children altogether, rejecting the choice of motherhood as a necessary function and a primary source of fulfillment for a woman, in contrast to the view promoted by more conservative traditional perspectives.

The intact two-parent, heterosexual family has become a less common phenomenon in modern society, to the extent that some consider it a social entity threatened by extinction. There are a number of reasons for this, which will be discussed in detail later in this chapter. At this point, let it suffice to say that the intact two-parent family is being supplanted in large numbers by alternative communal living units and living arrangements. These include single-parent families, communal settings in which a number of adults assume responsibility for a number of children without specific parental assignments, homosexual two-parent families which include children acquired both through adoption and artificial insemination, blended families consisting of a two-parent unit but including children of one or both parents from previous relationships, and a variety of other arrangements. The variations of arrangements and combinations reflects the overall transition in social and gender roles in recent years, and the experimentation in replacing unsatisfactory traditional institutions with alternative settings in search of more satisfactory arrangements. Society is undergoing a vast reorganization and restructuring because of the overall rise in awareness and consciousness in recent times, and the new ways of rethinking and envisioning gender relations and family structuring reflect this shift. Of course, many of these new experimental concepts produce less-than-satisfying results, which are publicized and widely criticized by fundamentalist clergymen and other defenders of traditional institutions. However, all these changes, successful and otherwise, represent the gradual state of flux through which the society of the future will emerge.

The advent of alternative living arrangements and the willingness to experiment with alternate lifestyles could not have gained the wide acceptance that it has without the change in social and spiritual consciousness that has gathered momentum since its emergence in the 1960's, and which also resulted in the dissatisfaction with traditional institutions during this period. With regard to the restructuring of the family unit, the disillusionment with the traditional family and its supporting values and concepts may be traced to and linked with the growing dissatisfaction with almost all established traditions that emerged in that era.

In earlier times, literary works like *Little House on the Prairie* and television programs like *Father Knows Best* and *Leave it to Beaver* extolled the virtues of family life based on patriarchal authority, and its role in each person's sense of security and life satisfaction. The complex concepts encapsulated in the term "family values" form the basis of ideological texts for conservative political and religious groups which view themselves as the defenders and champions of such traditions. Advocates and promoters of such groups trumpet the term on bumper stickers, t-shirts and billboards. But what do "traditional family values" in fact entail? All too often, they imply and encourage unquestioning submission to a paternal authority; adherence to a code of conduct that requires strict compliance without question; and a creation of roles that perpetuates stereotypical functions and values at the expense of individuality and creativity. Suppression of original—and non-conforming—thoughts and actions is essential, as these can cause "destructive" deviations from the "norm," and submission to the patriarchal authority is considered essential if the system is to function smoothly. This mindset is absolutely based on a "father knows best" mentality, which has as its logical extension the conclusion that all authority figures and institutions, such as churches, schools, government and the military all "know best," and are therefore to be followed with unquestioned loyalty and submission. The determination of who is "good" or "bad" is made according to the degree of adherence and conformity the individual displays; in fact, the person perceived as best is one who perceives oneself not at all as an individual, but rather as a component of a smoothly-functioning system.

Erving Goffman's classic work, *Asylums*, which examined the direction and quality of care given to institutionalized mental health patients in the 1960's, determined that the single most important criterion cited by therapists and staff in deciding that a patient had returned to "normal" and could be deemed ready for release was the ability to conform with and respond to staff expectations and directives. The standard for "normalcy" in our psychiatric hospitals is reflective of what the expectations are if one is to be successfully assimilated and able to function in society at large. In short, this is the basis for the authoritarian world view, one specifically designed to extinguish any trace of original thought, creative endeavor, or possibility of personal actualization.

In fact, the family unit—be it two or twenty in number—is a system, as is society at large. Everything acted out or initiated by one member affects all the other members, and everyone involved both affects and is affected by the actions, thoughts and energy of the others. In the traditional family model, the actions, functions and even thoughts of the members must be closely monitored and controlled, lest they interfere with the absolute control of the father over the whole. In this model, roles and functions are clearly defined and strictly enforced, although they aren't always articulated aloud. If one enters such a family, it can be quickly ascertained who is "smart," "cute," "shy," "a good sport," "tough," and so on. These are not just casual descriptions; they are carefully applied labels that strictly define role and function, to be strictly adhered to so as to meet expectations and cause a minimum of disruption to the functioning of the system. They may as well be uniforms each person wears! The more insidious function of these labels, however, is that they conceal the range of behaviors and personal modifications each person must make in order to fit into their assigned role. For example, the "hero child" of the family, the one who carries high expectations for achievement (honor student, athletic star, altar boy, accomplished musician) may find that pursuing ever-increasing levels of achievement leaves very little time or energy for play, reflection or self-awareness. Such a child often *becomes* his or her role, and is reluctant to display desires or behaviors that conflict with the family's role expectations.

The "model student, altar boy" type may feel ashamed in adolescence when confronted by his or her awakening sexual feelings, and may want to suppress these, with disastrous consequences in another area of life. Emotions are e-motions, or energy in motion moving outward, and therefore they can never be totally suppressed within. Since, as physics students know, energy can neither be created nor destroyed, it will surface in another place and time in one's life, usually as a compulsive behavior pattern. This kind of repression and subsequent acting-out is probably the motivation behind such behaviors as Sigmund Freud's cocaine abuse, Ernest Hemingway's alcoholism and suicide, or John Kennedy's extramarital indiscretions. The continued lack of opportunity to be around boys may cause an otherwise conservative young woman to go through periods of experimenting with sex and drugs once she's removed from the restrictive family environment. Conversely, children who are told that they're not as smart as some of their siblings, or that they're "no good at school," or any other such directives disguised as casual observations will also internalize and act out those roles.

The child who is not expected to be a good student will attain poor grades, often in spite of high scores on intelligence tests; the child expected to "get in trouble" will, even when faced with the prospect of corporal punishment or other severe consequences.

In *The Politics of Experience*, R. D. Laing talks about the baby who from infancy is said to be "the spitting image of his uncle," and from that day is subtly but carefully encouraged and groomed to adopt that uncle's attitudes and behavior patterns through the subtle and usually subconscious reinforcements of family members.

Families will often collude in order to coerce members to stay in their roles, or to conceal patterns or problems that don't coincide with the public image the family tries to project. It's common to hear about the break-up of a relationship accompanied by remarks such as "I can't believe it; they seemed like the perfect couple" by others conditioned within their own family to overlook underlying flaws in relationships.

A person whose homosexuality causes discomfort and embarrassment to the family may be described to outsiders as "shy and withdrawn," or "too busy with work" in explaining that person's lack of a heterosexual partner. A drug or alcohol problem may be explained away as "chronic fatigue" or "recurring illness" in attempting to rationalize the person's frequent social withdrawals or absences from the workplace. Emotional distance and avoidance among family members may be covered up by the excuses of dedication to work (workaholism) or commitment to the community (the excessive involvement in various clubs and projects that substitutes for satisfaction in personal relationships).

In such families, the cover-up of dysfunction and the necessary collusions and deceptions necessitate the expenditure of a good deal of energy, both physical and emotional. Yet the process of covering up the family's flaws remains a priority, and any member unwilling to play along or, worse still, willing to blow the whistle on the cover-up is regarded as a liability, and portrayed as "sick" or "deviant." Most psychiatric hospitals could not survive financially if they didn't accept and "treat" people whose most glaring "dysfunction" is rebelling and refusing to go along with a dysfunctional family system. Similarly, such hospitals also cater to patients whose very real problems, such as alcohol, drug abuse and depression, are the result of attempting to overlook or coexist with family system dysfunctions. Such compensations often must be extreme, because the dysfunctions they attempt to conceal are extreme. Families in which sexual abuse occurs often deny its existence, even though more than just the perpetrator and the victim(s) collude to both create the environment which allows the abusive situation to occur, as well as to cover it up. A common dynamic in father-daughter incest (by far the most prevalent type of incest in occurrence) is that the mother will often be aware of the sexual contact between father and daughter and will "turn the other way," or even actually promote its occurrence, rather than be forced to confront the emotional and sexual dysfunction in her own relationship with her husband. Similarly, it's common for mother and daughter in such a situation to act like jealous rivals towards each other, while all the time outwardly denying that incest is occurring.

There may be some truth to the claim that the dissolution of the traditional nuclear family is behind a great many of society's ills, but this may ignore the greater truth: the dissolution of the traditional nuclear family has come about to a great extent due to a societal spiritual awakening, and a resulting reaffirmation of the individual's worth. In the wake of this movement, a system which promotes patriarchal authority and conformity at the expense of creativity and personal actualization *deserves* to go the way of the dinosaur, the dodo bird and the Edsel. (This shift in the societal order was reflected in the arts by plays such as *Hair, Oh, Calcutta!* and *Godspell,* and by television programs like *All in the Family.*) It is true that, as social human beings, we need support and sustenance from one another, and we need the healthy interdependence of a greater social unit; but it is absolutely essential that this unit also be a healthy unit.

"Healthy" means that it cannot be authoritarian, it cannot subvert the value of the individual, it cannot extinguish creativity, and cannot provide an environment in which disease, abuse and dysfunction may flourish. It must be democratic, supportive, and sensitive to the needs of each and every one of its members; and it must promote and encourage individual differences and variances as long as no one is flourishing at the expense of someone else. It cannot be patriarchal (or matriarchal, for that matter), racist, sexist, homophobic, or otherwise dogmatic. It must be a true family, based on acceptance, the ready and unconditional inclusion of all members, and the joyous, loving and guilt-free release of those ready to take off on a new path. It cannot be based strictly on biological heredity, but rather on communal inclusion, nurturing and a sense of belonging.

We are a long way from the proliferation of such families, and if the concept sounds too "pie in the sky," that may say more about how far away we are from attaining such an ideal as a society, than how attainable and viable it actually is.

Chapter 6

Educational Systems

For many people and cultures, education is considered *the* crucial key to success. They believe that the longer you study, the more you know, and the greater the number of professional initials behind your name, the better your chances for wealth, recognition and all the other trappings that we include in the more common definitions of "success." Many ethnic and cultural groups identify this belief as central to their group image, a sort of collective "I think (and study), therefore I am." In reality, however, nothing could be further from the truth! Academic titles and credentials are routinely attained by people who are completely incompetent in the actual practice of their profession. One of my first clinical supervisors in graduate school was a man who had both his Bachelor's and Doctoral degrees from a very prestigious Ivy League institution, with a perfect 4.0 average, and was about as involved and effective in a therapy session as a piece of furniture! The man had the intellectual understanding of all the principles and processes to go with his impeccable academic credentials, but he couldn't *do* what he was trying to teach us to save his life!

Conversely, many people have allowed their lack of formal education, or their perceived lack of opportunity for attaining it, to hold them back from perceiving their dream and vocation. They allow irrelevant and unrealistic beliefs and assumptions, like "no one in my family has ever gone to college, so how can I think that I could go?" or "to do that requires four more years of education, and I don't have either the time or the money," to stop them from pursuing their calling. They forget that their capacity to achieve something has nothing to do with anyone else around them, and that for someone with a dream there *are* no limitations—except self-imposed ones. As the eastern sages remind us, "argue for your limitations, and they are yours!" If you really want something, the opportunity and necessary funding will be found. The very desire to do something indicates that you already have the native ability. All that ability needs is to be allowed into the light of day, and perhaps some relatively narrow refinement(s)! Each and every one of us can achieve anything that we set our minds to, and allow our desires to expand towards. Jesus Himself said, "the least among you can do all that I have, and more." Think about that. Someone Who performed miracles, raised the dead, and influenced the world as no one else has, saying to us that the *least* among us has His powers, and more! What greater testimonial to the infinity of human potential can you have than that?

Formal education, then, is not the key to happiness and success it was supposed to be. In many cases, it's a hindrance to the very access to opportunity and personal growth it was meant to develop and provide, in spite of what the expensive television ads that are broadcast on behalf of many colleges and vocational schools would lead you to believe. It's true that many professions cannot be practiced without a certain amount of formal training, but stop to think: if such training was really essential to the practice of the profession, would anyone have to legally compel you to undergo the training in order to practice? For many decades, quite a number of states allowed one to sit for the bar exam—necessary to the practice of law in that state—without requiring any formal training in accredited law schools. It wasn't until those schools realized they were losing tuition revenues, and formally trained lawyers faced stiff competition from such self-educated colleagues, that formal training in the law was established as a prerequisite for taking the bar exam. This is largely due to the nature of the process. In the attempt to indoctrinate students into its systemic rules and regulations, organized society must also provide them with limits regarding what is "acceptable" and what is to be avoided with regard to one's behavior, aspirations, social standing, and even personal thoughts and feelings.

The system's many measuring sticks for the success of such indoctrination, such as grades, examinations, or intelligence and achievement tests, measure the individual's capacity to conform to a system and a set of standards. The ability to perform well on scholastic examinations measures absorption and conformity of thought to material presented in the classroom much more than any innate talent, ability or capacity for original thought. The truth is that our society, in its dread of the power and lack of regimentation that an unleashing of unrestricted thought might produce, has attempted to limit and restrict such a possibility by rewarding conformity, while discouraging, sometimes by severe measures, creativity and originality. One of the ways to accomplish this is to set very narrow restrictions on the ways that one may acquire knowledge and training, as well as the amount of formal training which is required to formally confirm one's competency in a particular area or profession. More damaging has been the corollary belief that anything worth having must be attained only as a result of hard work and according to prescribed guidelines, often voiced as "if we had to go through it, *you* have to go through it," a precept expounded by defenders of traditional institutions.

Perhaps the most important single factor inhibiting the effectiveness and limiting the potential of formal education is its rigid structure. This structure manifests itself in two important ways, both of which are very damaging to the likelihood that many students will derive maximum benefit from their educational experience; these two factors are present from kindergarten through college. One of these factors is most school administrators' insistence on a "well-rounded curriculum," which exposes students to subjects in which they have little interest, and in which they therefore show little aptitude. The second limiting factor is the insistence on grades as a measure of progress, but also as a comparative measure of scholastic aptitude among students.

The practice of exposing students to subjects which hold little interest for them, in the interest of exposing them to a complete curriculum, seems primarily motivated by a desire to maintain educators from a wide spectrum of disciplines gainfully employed. It needlessly burdens many students with facts and concepts which are of little interest or use to them, and dampen their overall interest in continued studies. Those among my readers who remember memorizing declentions of Latin verbs, the date of the Missouri Compromise, or the process for determining geometric proofs as parts of their required curriculum may be able to relate to the burden of unnecessary information confronting students in the current system. Some early exposure to a variety of subjects may help students to discover where their interests and aptitudes lie. Beyond that, after some basics of grammar, arithmetic, etc., in the early grades, there is really no necessity to burden students with "required" subjects throughout their academic career. In fact, allowing students to choose a curriculum entirely consisting of topics which truly interest them might raise the current tepid level of interest in school attendance and participation to presently unimaginable levels, reversing today's alarming drop-out statistics.

Within such a reformed academic environment, there would still be a place for classical scholars to study Homer and Virgil, or future historians to discuss the factors leading to the Spanish-American War. However, think of the incredible levels of originality, creativity and enthusiasm for learning if we allowed our young people to not only dream of but begin actually training to become the next Emily Dickinson, John Steinbeck, Albert Camus, Neil Simon, Meryl Streep, Rodin, Ruth Bader Ginsburg, Picasso, I. M. Pei, Mozart, or Christiaan Barnard even before the onset of adolescence! Instead, in the current system students are bogged down by the requirement to complete studies unrelated to their interests all the way through college, where such required courses greatly outnumber the courses in their major area of study and electives combined! It's no wonder that so many young people abandon their education prematurely, or that so many choose to escape what they regard as "the ivory tower" of academia for "the real world." It isn't until graduate school that students are allowed to pursue a course of study completely devoted to their area of interest, and by that time the majority of students, including many of "the best and the brightest," have left to pursue their life away from a system that doesn't respond to their interests, and fails to stimulate their imagination. The fact that so many people in our culture pursue careers in which the actual tasks of the position are of little interest to them may be the one lasting residual impression about life expectations left on them by their academic experiences.

The second factor which contaminates enthusiasm for the educational process, the use of grades as an indicator of relative success or progress, is equally damaging to student enthusiasm for learning. Grades ideally could be used to indicate relative progress for each student, and to help them determine their areas of interest for continued study. As they are currently used in schools, however, grades do a lot more harm than good by creating inhibiting pressure and performance anxiety, and in damaging many students' self-esteem and confidence. Because the vast majority of students cannot be competent in all areas of the curriculum, the lower grades in their weaker subjects often serve to remind them of their fallibility and undermine their confidence, thus often also serving as harbingers of future failures. Students with a narrow range of interests and/or competence may come to develop a view of themselves as failures due to the greater number of lower grades, dissuading them from continued study in their areas of interest. Even students who earn high grades may be seduced by the competition among their peers (which educators, parents and prospective institutions of higher learning tend to encourage) into pursuing higher grades at the expense of true learning, thus sacrificing the full development of their talents. Thus, attention to grades at best deflects students from the true purpose of learning, and at worst discourages extended participation in academia. It is not that our students are failing in greater numbers; it is that the school system, as it is currently structured and applied from the first year through college, is failing the vast majority of its participants.

Even our concepts of sociopolitical structure and direction have been severely limited and compromised. Whereas in the original model of democracy, classical Athens, the individual was encouraged to participate directly and to be responsible in the exercise of his civic and political duties by becoming educated and adequately informed, the modern so-called democracies and republics pay lip service to individual participation and instead encourage conformity, providing only a limited number of parties and representatives appointed to do the voting and, presumably, the thinking for their constituents. True, in ancient Athens women were excluded from the political process; but in modern society gender discrimination has been gradually replaced by intellectual and spiritual limitations. Rather than being provided an equal opportunity to achieve individual excellence, we are bought off with the pabulum of equal mediocrity. We are fed the illusions of security promoted by slogans such as "all men are created equal," "a chicken in every pot," and "security from the cradle to the grave." We are encouraged towards immediate gratification and relief from stress and discomfort which are, more often than not, themselves artificially manufactured. Our young are indoctrinated in the comfortable indulgence of television, including MTV and the mind-numbing, shallow programming offered on most stations, while their parents content themselves with soap operas, videos and sports. We are slowly being transformed into a society of passive, intellectually sterile and lazy dolts. We respond to trite slogans about religion, family and patriotism rather than seeking true education and exercising original thought. Our socialization and training have influenced us to prefer the false temporary security of a six-pack and a square meal to mental stimulation and spiritual development. Instead of a social climate encouraging intellectual development and inquiry by all, we separate the intellectually active among us as a minority of elite persons, separate and alien from the "common man" who, as my grandfather used to say, has become far too common!

The relative scarcity of well-educated and intellectually developed people in our society is not just an unfortunate circumstance, or a consequence of an educational system that just happens to be deficient in comparison to its European or Japanese counterparts. Those who decry the deficiencies of American schools and look forward to reforms which will bring our schools in line with their foreign counterparts would be well advised to not hold their breath while waiting for these reforms. There is a wide disparity between the quality of education offered to the children of the wealthy and socially prominent in this country, and that offered to the children of the majority of the population, and this disparity is quite intentional. This is true from the kindergarten level through the universities. Such a policy is hardly surprising in a society which shows little value for the quality of life of the average person, also reflected in inadequate gun control laws and woefully inadequate public health care.

Simply put, the masses are undereducated and inadequately prepared to compete at the highest levels of business and government, because the elite who hold the reins of power and wealth are loath to share access to their advantaged status with the *hoi polloi*. Instead, the power elite want to perpetuate the existence of a wide base of undereducated and underachieving class with limited aspirations for its own future. In my experiences as a volunteer in the public school system, I encountered students in the schools within affluent neighborhoods who aspired to college educations and professional careers. Their counterparts in poverty-stricken districts aspired to careers in sports or in the drug trade, and perhaps to surviving until their late twenties if they failed to get out of their neighborhood. This lack of adequate preparation and limited expectations are perhaps most accurately reflected in the role models chosen by children from poor communities and minority populations. Too many of them fantasize about becoming professional athletes or entertainers; far fewer aspire to professional or civic careers.

Such a perpetual cheap human resource may be continually used and exploited as a poorly compensated, functional slave labor base used to support and maintain the existing power structure with its efforts. This wider population labor base requires only the barest maintenance and support in terms of inadequate education, meager economic compensation and bare-bones health care in order to be enlisted in serving the interests of the powerful.

Intellectual capability is no longer portrayed as the accessible right of all, but a privilege of the educated elite among us, yet is somehow separate from the mainstream of our society. The "thinkers" among us are almost exclusive to this separate caste, and so we no longer have many thinking and inquiring bricklayers (like Socrates), carpenters (like Jesus), or even political leaders (like Marcus Aurelius, Abraham Lincoln or John Kennedy). We have political lobbies to tell us how to vote, talk shows to tell us how to feel and think, churches to provide us with beliefs and moral guidelines, schools to narrowly train but not truly educate us, and jobs to keep us occupied and provided with just enough compensation to continue in this dreary cycle. In the process, we immerse ourselves in a perpetual stupor that dissolves any awareness of who we are and what our lives are really all about. Instead of being in touch with the spirituality that is the essence of our being, we focus on driving the right car, living in the right neighborhood, wearing clothing with the right labels, smoking and drinking the "in" substances, and conforming, conforming, conforming.

How does all this start? Back in the 1960's, R. D. Laing pointed to the spiritual, intellectual and emotional violence performed on each and every one of us from birth. In his seminal work first published in 1967, *The Politics of Experience*, Laing asserted that "the family is a legalized system for doing violence on one another," just one of the radical statements that earned him his status as a maverick and extremist in the eyes of the mainstream psychiatric establishment of the era. Laing was excoriated for such opinions by that same establishment, but most of his views have been largely vindicated by the family therapy movement a generation later. In fact, the ever-increasing awareness about family dysfunction and its effect on society makes one wonder if the really dangerous radicals are not the ministers and defenders of the system. From early on, children are told what to feel, how and when to express it, what to believe, whom to be associated with, what to aspire to, and what should be considered beyond their grasp. In the process, they are taught and encouraged to internalize a ponderous litany of "shoulds," beginning with never disagreeing with or being angry at adults, never questioning certain established beliefs such as the existence of God or the assumed superiority of capitalism over communism, and conforming to certain rules of conduct. They emerge with a clearly defined, but very unrealistic and limiting world view, on which they rely to determine whom they should marry, how much education and which profession to pursue, and what regulations and limits to respect and observe. In the process, they slash and burn so much of their true nature that they *become* their amalgam of roles at the expense of a loss of identity and feelings of dissatisfaction with their lives. Some try to recover at least some of this loss of self-awareness with hobbies, seminars and workshops, or psychotherapy; others turn to chemicals (smoking, drugs, alcohol) or behavioral addictions (sex, gambling) to sedate their awareness of their spiritual emptiness.

An ever-increasing number of people abandon their "successful" pursuits in mid-life to pursue less complex, but more personally meaningful lifestyles. They are returning to school to study subjects that really interest them, supplementing the "practical" studies of their youth, which provided them entry into the work force, but left their souls untouched. Whereas such changes were viewed with cynicism and suspicion in the past, mid-life career changes have become common and gained acceptance as more and more people no longer choose to be bound by rules and expectations set for them by others in their past. Changes in vocation and career are available to everyone, as are educational and spiritual studies that in the past were dismissed as impractical or unrealistic. The only limits to following your dream and expanding your awareness are the ones that you place on yourself. There is an abundance of outlets and resources to provide you with all you want and need in this regard, assuming that you're willing to ask for and pursue it, and allow for its manifestation into your life. Yes, it may mean that you may have to push some current interests or obligations aside in order to make your pursuit of your dreams a priority; but then, placing yourself first is a prerequisite towards satisfaction in life and personal growth. This premise stands in contrast to the moral and religious training many in our society receive, which teaches that to put oneself first is selfish and vain. In truth, by caring for yourself first, you will be more satisfied, better motivated, and more focused in your capacity to know and develop your resources and make them available to others. By contrast, consistently putting your own needs and desires "on the back burner" will provide you with little satisfaction, deplete your mental and physical resources due to "deficit spending" in those areas, and render you largely ineffective and useless to others due to dissatisfaction and burnout.

Don't believe that a lack of formal education or funding can prevent you from meeting your personal or professional aspirations. All of us know of someone who started with very little money and became a huge business success, perhaps partly because that person didn't have the expertise to be aware of the risks and pitfalls involved that working through an MBA degree would have made him/her aware of. We also know very educated people "trapped" within the false security of a corporate job, who despise their existence, but can see no "responsible" alternative.

I was supervised as a graduate student by a terrific teacher and therapist, who at age 39 found herself widowed with three young children, no money and no training, and who at 48 had a Ph.D. in social work, a healthy private practice, and a life she had never considered attainable while her husband was still alive.

Recently, I resided in a state which required no specific education or training for psychotherapists, and shared office space with a woman who worked as a counselor although she had completed only one year of college. She happened to be a very talented therapist, and achieved a yearly six-figure income, which she richly deserved. Again, there seems to be no correlation between formal training and ability; therefore, don't let others tell you what is or is not available to you because of your age, gender or education. All such negative people do is infect you with their beliefs about limitations and expectations. Be very careful about buying into their logic or thinking in this regard. If you want to do something, go do it; if you need certain resources, they will become available to you, if you are willing to ask for them *and believe that you deserve them!* It doesn't matter *how* such resources reach you; very often, you yourself won't know. But you live in an abundant universe, and it will provide you with all you need, for the asking!

The great doctor, teacher and philosopher, Deepak Chopra, tells of going with Maharishi Mahesh Yogi to a conference at which the Maharishi was promoting a world peace project. According to Dr. Chopra, when a skeptic in the audience asked the Maharishi where all the money for such an ambitious project was to come from, he replied without hesitation, "from wherever it is at the moment." The Maharishi knew that money, like all other resources in the universe, is available in boundless quantities; moreover, it is there for the asking by anyone who believes him or herself worthy of receiving it. You too can have what you ask for, and *all* you ask for; if you don't get it, or don't get it in the amount or form you requested, the person standing between you and the fulfillment of your request is in your mirror. Change your mindset about what you really want and deserve, and it will be yours. And for God's sake, don't deprive yourself of your dreams because someone without your vision attempts to contaminate you with *their* lack of vision or confidence. I learned this lesson in dramatic fashion, when I was facilitating a therapy group for people with AIDS. One of the recurring issues was the resistance of many young people who, until recently, had been healthy and symptom-free to apply for and accept disability benefits; most of them expressed reluctance towards receiving such payments, because in their view their current good health could not "justify" what they regarded as a waste of public funds. Some also expressed the concern that accepting disability benefits would influence them to consider themselves as handicapped, and thus facilitate the onset of symptoms of the disease, as well as cause them to think of themselves as less worthy of survival. It wasn't until one young man stood up in a session and declared that he had also entertained such feelings and thoughts initially, but had come to realize that the benefits were really "*deserve*ability payments" that would enable him to live better and longer, that this became an irrelevant issue for the group.

You don't need an MBA to be successful in business, you don't need a Ph.D. to be a terrific counselor, and you don't need a "good" (read: "practical") reason to study literature, basketweaving, archaeology, art, French, ancient history, or thermonuclear physics. Don't be influenced or limited by common socially-fostered stereotypes: A professional woman need not "balance" her career with child-rearing in order to feel "complete," someone born to a poor family need not accept perpetual poverty as one's lot in life, a male of large physical stature need not take an interest in athletics, and someone born into a wealthy family has no automatic pass to happiness and life satisfaction. All of us must respond to our circumstances, but none of us are bound to or by those circumstances. Tell yourself your dream, and then go for it. If you don't get it the first time, or the third, or the twenty-third, go for it again!

Those who really love you in your life will support you and do what they can to help you along (assuming you're not being self-destructive, as in the active indulgence of an addiction). Those who try to dissuade and discourage you because they don't believe in your dream (or because your dream is better than theirs) are not your real friends, and you don't need them along your life's journey anyway. Send them away in love, but send them! The only real security is the willingness to get up again and keep trying, and the only real failure is quitting and doing nothing! Go for it; you have nothing to lose but your inhibitions and limitations! Don't ever worry about ultimately not getting it. In the heart of every failure is the seed of your ultimate success; the world is one big smorgasbord, if you'll only walk up with your plate.

Chapter 7

Spirituality and Religious Institutions

Religion, or a belief in a "Presence" greater than Man, is probably as old as the human race itself. The overly simplistic explanation usually given about religion's origins, that primitive man "invented" gods and the supernatural in order to create some foundation for the natural events he couldn't otherwise explain or understand, may provide part of the reason for the founding of religion, or more correctly, the discovery of the divine by man. This is not a completely adequate explanation, however. The more complete explanation is that natural phenomena beyond man's ability to explain or rationally understand gave him an awareness of an existence that was greater than himself, which he then attempted to internalize and anthropomorphize through myth and religious constructs.

With the development of communities and social structure, it wasn't long before commonly held beliefs and customs
crystallized into organized religion. Tribal and national leaders
quickly recognized that supporting their authority by presenting it as a logical consequence and integral part of the divine
order gave their directives greater clout, and removed any
momentum or appearance of legitimacy from opposing factions. In some societies, such as ancient Egypt, the ruler was
presented as an incarnate manifestation of the supreme deity,
so that to oppose the ruler was to blaspheme against the divine.
Less direct but equally effective manifestations of this practice,
such as the "divine right" of kings and the assumed providential
endorsement of certain rulers and dictators, survive to this day.
We are all too familiar with opposing sides in wars who both
claim to have God on their side. This desire of rulers to present
themselves as divinely ordained and supported in order to
suppress any opposition or questioning of their authority
naturally led to a working relationship between rulers and
clergy. It was a case of mutual need; the clergy needed the
support and protection of the ruler in order to operate unhin-
dered and to eliminate competing faiths, while the ruler needed
the endorsement of the clergy to render any opposition to his
authority "illegitimate" and therefore ineffective. In many
cases, this partnership led to the establishment of a state
religion, which meant that to promote any set of contrary
beliefs was to be guilty of treason as well as blasphemy! It would

take some very determined opposition to risk being found guilty of that level of transgression.

The partnership of rulers and the clergy afforded both incredible control over the populace they commanded. They not only had control of a person's behavior and fate in this existence, but well into the next! They reasoned, quite correctly in most cases, that few would risk transgressing the code of conduct laid out by church and state when to do so would mean not only punishment of the body in this life, but punishment of the soul in the afterlife as well. It was with such an application in mind that, in one example, concepts like Purgatory and Hell were devised. It was this manufactured illusion of controlling a person even beyond the grave that also gave both church and state greater access to the pocketbook of the common man; the church could demand additional taxes, known as "tithes," which provided care and maintained a person's soul in good standing, much as taxes paid to the state provided services and protection in this life. In addition, paying fines for moral transgressions, even after a person's death, was believed to redeem a person's soul in the afterlife, and gain them a place in a better eternal home. If this concept sounds similar to the upgrade in traveling or lodging facilities that many airlines and hotels offer conditionally, that's no coincidence. The same good business sense that went into the latter also inspired the former. As P. T. Barnum could have said, "there's a pious believer born every minute."

Through the gullibility of the believers and the threat of eternal suffering imposed on them for failure to comply, many churches and religions amassed considerable financial and political power, which they used to impose their dictates on both the state and the individual. The necessity to promote—and have people be willing to pay for—a service they were originally not aware they needed is exemplified by the paired concepts of salvation and damnation that the churches invented in order to create the populace's dependency on their blessing and guidance. The single most outrageous invention used to facilitate the implementation of this notion is the idea of "original sin." As Stuart Wilde so wittily observed, they probably called it that because it was such an *original* idea for drawing in and creating this artificial dependency in millions of believers—who, once they were convinced that they were by their very nature damaged, deficient and evil, would then do whatever was required to secure salvation including, of course, paying for the privilege over and over again. It works well, too; millions upon millions of people have been influenced by their religious training and convictions to go through life feeling flawed and incomplete, because along with their human traits they have this contrived "original sin" hanging around their necks. They then perceive no alternative but to appeal to their church to save them from this artificially created, self-imposed burden. Is there anything more criminal than to have institutions which are supposedly devoted to spiritual development and enlightenment instead imposing such a damaging, self-defeating concept on their adherents? And for what? So that they can maintain their followers' dependency and convince them that they are sinful, worthless, damned, "damaged goods" due for an eternity of judgment and punishment unless the religious institution can intercede on their behalf. In this manner, they continue to drain their adherents financially for a false service—salvation—that they didn't need in the first place! This rivals the manufacture and marketing of cigarettes as the most successful promotion of a harmful and completely unnecessary commodity in history!

Reincarnation, the development and evolution of a soul through multiple lives, is not a concept introduced by and confined to eastern religions. Christianity included it for many centuries, until the Middle Ages. It was probably around that time that someone within the Church figured out that allowing people to believe in reincarnation was contrary to the political and economic best interests of the Church. After all, if every soul were here to experience and evolve spiritually, and all experiences were part of that process (not needing, therefore, to be judged as "good" or "evil"), there would be then no need for people to fear their fate or to dread their place in an afterlife. Instead, the Church promoted the concept of a single incarnation, at the end of which each person would be at the mercy of a deity which would judge one's life, and assign each soul to a heaven, hell or purgatory—all according to how closely that person's life had adhered to the teachings and guidance of the Church. Thus, the Church could assume a controlling role in people's lives, and dangle the threat of a judgmental and punitive deity before them to ensure their compliance. Further, the Church could then present itself as having "the inside track" to salvation, and offer ways in which the "sinful" could purchase their way out of hell and back into the deity's good graces. By use of this concept, the Church greatly enriched itself, and expanded its political influence; but it also increased the anxiety and pathology of its followers, who now saw themselves as inherently flawed and sinful. In the process, people's capacity to enjoy life and fulfill their dreams was greatly curtailed, and the joy and creativity which are everyone's birthright were just as greatly restricted. Natural, carefree enjoyment of relationships, sexuality and life were replaced by conformity to a restrictive and punitive "morality" which has filled so many lives with fear and dread of judgment and punishment, and deprived people of joy in daily living and awareness of their inherent divine nature.

The modern practice of psychiatry, which has identified and "treats" so many varieties of emotional and psychological symptoms, owes a great debt to the Church's invention of a punitive and judgmental deity, which has induced people to function out of guilt and dread instead of joy and wonder. Almost all of psychiatry's "pathology" stems from the unnecessary pressure people feel to deny and contain themselves, so as not to offend the god who will confirm their flawed nature and assign them to eternal torture and pain. If people will recover their awareness of their own divine nature, and in the process shed their attachment to judgment and guilt, the creativity and joy thus released will create a level of bliss to surpass any religious concept of a heaven. As Wayne Dyer points out, each of us is punished not *for* our judgment and guilt, but *by* our judgment and guilt. Get rid of such corrosive concepts, and rejoice in the eternal bliss which is your nature and your birthright! *The Course in Miracles* tells us that the Last Judgment is not some dreaded final exam which will assign the fortunate few to heaven and the many flawed and sinful to their punishment; it is the final relinquishing of *all* judgment and the need to judge, following which all will be free to live, love, create, and revel in their place within wondrous Creation, and the divinity within us all. You don't have to earn your salvation or your place within the divinity of creation. You are already in It, and It is in you, and no other person or institution can take It from you or you from It. To the extent that you still adhere to concepts such as judgment, punishment, injustice and tragedy, you are displaying your spiritual ignorance and deprivation. When the world realizes that there is nothing to be rewarded or punished, and our happiness and unhappiness are their own causes and consequences, the freedom of feeling and expression unleashed will create a paradise on earth far exceeding anything Milton or Dante could portray or even imagine.

Of course, the partnership between church and state was not always a smooth or amiable one. With so much power and control at stake, good ol' human nature sometimes took over from common sense and common interest, causing rulers and clergy to wrestle for ultimate control. The history books are replete with examples of both using their "divine right" to justify pushing the other into the background. In ancient Egypt, high priests could and did order the removal of Pharaohs from the throne, when said Pharaohs even hinted that they would attempt to subvert the priests' authority. Since "living gods" like the Pharaohs didn't have much of a retirement plan, what could they do? Refer to themselves as "god emeritus" and write books, or go on talk shows or the lecture tour? Involuntary passage into the next level of existence through assassination disguised as a sudden illness was devised. Records of the time confirm the repeated application of this practice, which must have surely given the high priests the upper hand in any potential power struggle with the succeeding Pharaoh.

More recently, the Catholic Church used its influence to promote the Crusades, the Spanish Inquisition, and endorsed the rule of both Hitler and Mussolini in exercising its policy of eliminating conflicting belief systems and gaining further control over its adherents with threats of torture, execution and excommunication. When heads of state would oppose the Church's directives, the threat of excommunication would be used to pull the dissenting ruler back in line, with the double threat of removing divine endorsement from his rule and condemning his soul, and the souls of any loyal adherents, to damnation and the tortures of hell.

When the Church tried this with Henry VIII of England, he responded by throwing Catholic clerics out of his nation, and establishing his own church—the Anglican, or Episcopal Church. The threat of excommunication did not deter Martin Luther from establishing Protestant Christianity, either. Even the Vatican couldn't fool all of the people, all of the time.

The Moslem conquests of the sixth and seventh centuries were promoted as "jihads" (holy wars), with eternal bliss in Paradise offered to any of the faithful who fell in battle. In our own times, terrorists supporting Islamic causes have killed and/or forfeited their own lives freely, in their belief that their cause and faith justified their killing and provided bliss for them in the afterlife.

In our own society, the separation of church and state has not been as complete as the Founding Fathers had envisioned. Churches and religious factions influence political races, attempt to formally legislate their views of morality, and even oppose certain scientific advances, all in the pursuit of maintaining the status quo and their control over their followers. Religious groups in recent history have attempted to suppress the finding that the earth is *not* the center of the solar system; to attempt banning the teaching of the theory of evolution in the public schools; to oppose integration and interracial relationships; to promote discrimination against gays and lesbians; to prevent life-enhancing medicines and devices from becoming readily available, such as condoms and RU486 (the "abortion pill"); to rationalize wars and the virtual extermination of certain ethnic groups (the Jews in Europe during the Holocaust and the native Americans in the United States, in the name of white Christian "Manifest Destiny").

Organized religion, like organized crime, is intended to control and direct, while enriching itself and its beneficiaries. Is it any wonder that these two institutions so often find themselves aligned to support the same issues and causes? Don't give over your personal power capacity for independent thought to some religious group or organization—much less your money.

The original Greek word for "church," *ekklesia*, means a communion of people, a coming together in spirit. This is what a church and religion are intended to be, rather than totalitarian systems that control through threats and applied guilt. In particular, give a very wide berth to any person or institution claiming to be "the one and only" pathway to the divine. All truly enlightened spiritual traditions freely acknowledge the divinity of all and the many paths available to the Light. Anyone who claims sole proprietorship of the path to enlightenment or salvation is instead trying to control and ensnare people into trading their awareness and self-love for dependence and subservience.

You are an incarnate manifestation of the divine, as we all are. As Wayne Dyer reminds us, we are not basically human beings having sporadic spiritual experiences; we are spiritual beings, having a human experience. This world is our current level of existence, but it is not our Home. We will return Home on the happy occasion of our exit from this world of illusion, which we call "death," and which many of us dread because we have forgotten our true, eternal essence.

You are perfect as you are, and whatever you are, have done or are becoming has occurred for a myriad of reasons, *all of them* contributing to your spiritual development (although that may not always be obvious to your human mind as things occur to you). There is nothing to forgive, nothing to atone for, nothing and no one in need of salvation; it's all part of a perfect, divine plan. Go on with your life, live and let live, let others come into or out of your life as you and they please, but always join with and let go of them in a spirit of love.

Accept life's bounty and be generous with yourself *first*, so that you will then have both the resources and the security to be generous with others. If others come along to attempt to indoctrinate you in a set of beliefs that involve giving up some of your power, self-esteem or self-image, send them away in love, but don't permit them to keep chipping away at you.

Remember Deepak Chopra's account of the response a Vedic wise man gave to a religious fundamentalist who accused him of being an atheist: "I used to not believe in God, until I realized that I *am* God." When the spiritual master was then challenged to affirm or deny Christ's divinity, he responded, "I wouldn't ever deny *anyone's* divinity."

Our access to the divine is infinite, and our capacity to access this unlimited resource can be the pathway to having and manifesting any situation, any relationship, any condition in our lives. Do you believe that you have ordered the circumstances of your life as it is right now? You have! Can you change any or all of them at any time ? Of course; all you have to do is ask, tap into the divine source that is continually flowing through you. "Ask and ye shall receive; knock on the door, and it will be opened to you." Jesus' instructions are as true today as they have always been, and equally true for every single person on the planet. We are the most powerful creating creatures in the universe, yet we are encouraged by persons and institutions who wish to control us to believe in the limits of our creative capacity, and forget that we have infinite access to God's bounty. All we have to do is ask, and it is ours for the asking. All we need is to instruct the Universe, and It cannot help but accede to our wishes.

So many are reluctant to access their divinity and creativity, because they have come to believe the limiting religious and political institutions that preach submission, insecurity, guilt, and dependency on supposedly more powerful and more deserving people outside oneself, who are consequently assumed to have greater or easier access to the divine. You don't need such intercession on your behalf by anyone, and there is no one more capable of communing with the divine than you. Your "higher power" is not out there somewhere, it is within you, and always has been. You *are* divine by your very nature, remember? So ask away, and expect to receive what you ask for merely for asking. Don't let some person or institution talk you out of your birthright! Remember Lily Tomlin's witty inquiry: "why is it that when you talk to God it's called prayer, but when God talks to you it's called schizophrenia?" The communication line with God is wide open in both directions, and all you have to do is use it!

If you want to live consistently with the divine and the higher purpose within you, simply ask yourself "how may I serve?" A myriad ways are available to you for enhancing the lot of your fellow man, and that is a true ministry, a coming together in spirit. It is the path that truly divinely inspired people like Albert Schweitzer, Mother Teresa, Martin Luther King and Louise Hay have chosen and are choosing. Don't be dismayed or dissuaded from your path by your own enjoyment of your direction or purpose, deceived by the common misconception that worthy pursuits necessarily involve pain and struggle. All people throughout history who have used their skills and ideas to benefit their fellow man, the spiritual Masters of all traditions, have done so primarily out of the motivation to feel good for themselves and about themselves, *without exception*. We are at our best when we are acting to benefit ourselves, and necessarily must improve the lot of others when we nurture our self first. This is not selfish, so much as it is self-ful, willing to be filled with the divine spark within us and the divine spirit that guides our lives.

Let me close this section with an anecdote from the life of Adlai Stevenson, one of the truly intellectually gifted and inspired men of our time, in order to put this issue of our spiritual nature in perspective. It is said that Mr. Stevenson was tending to his farm, when the minister of his church was passing by in his carriage, and stopped to remark, "Brother Stevenson, you and the Lord have certainly cultivated a beautiful farm!"

Without hesitation, Stevenson responded, "Thank you, Reverend, but you ought to see what this place looked like when the Lord had it all by Himself!"

Chapter 8

Sexuality

Sexuality is the one area that causes more intense emotions and more conflicts between motivation and inhibition than any other area of human experience, especially in modern American society. American culture has separated and alienated sexuality so far from the rest of the human experience as to leave many people confused and unable to function in a natural and normal manner when it comes to this most fundamental and rewarding of human experiences. This is in stark contrast to most European societies, as well as many "underdeveloped" nations, in which sexual activity is accepted as a natural and normal part of life, and no particular efforts are made to restrict it, regulate it, or compartmentalize it through professional analysis, labeling and categorizing.

As the old saying goes, "what you resist, persists." In American society, sexuality is alternately repressed, unrealistically exalted, and inevitably distorted. What is culturally acceptable and appropriate is often emphasized over what comes naturally and is healthy, with the result that the individual—regardless of sexual identity, gender, or age—remains confused in the attempt to reconcile one's feelings with more widely accepted norms and standards.

Freud pointed to the sex drive as the primary motivator for all human behavior, whether that behavior is overtly sexual or not. He may have gone a bit overboard in placing such emphasis exclusively on the sexual drive, or libido, but there is no denying that it is a primary biological and psychological motivator, and that a person's sexual functioning is an important indicator of overall physical and emotional health status. I had a history professor in college who once remarked that "more of history has been determined in the bedroom than on all the battlefields in the world," and I suspect that this remark is remarkably close to the truth. Because of its strong influence on overall human behavior, sexuality has been scrutinized, categorized, judged and labeled in an effort to bring it under societal control, and harness its power over our thoughts and actions.

Ancient societies, especially the matriarchal tribes of early Indo-European history and tradition, celebrated sexuality and fertility as divine gifts to the human race. Both religious and political institutions freely acknowledged the role of sex in not only propagating the race, but also in making life pleasurable and comfortable. Fertility rites were central in religious rituals, and entire festivals were planned (usually coinciding with the planting of crops in the spring) to celebrate the ecstasy of the union of seed and field, the initiation of the reproductive cycle. In many ancient matriarchal societies, the queen (who was the ultimate ruler of the tribe or city) was publicly mated with an eligible male, and the purpose of making their sexual union a public spectacle had a dual purpose: it removed any doubt as to the legitimacy of the resulting heir to the throne, and it encouraged the general populace to celebrate and rejoice in the reaffirmation of sexuality as a desirable, sanctioned part of their own life. In many of these cultures, the queen would take on a new mate at the beginning of each year, so as to ensure a continued supply of young, healthy, virile males from whom the next generation of rulers would be conceived. (Some such tribes required the ritual sacrifice of the previous king by his replacement, in an effort to ensure that no rivalry or conflict would ensue, as well as to use the past king's blood to symbolically nurture the new year's crop. In some such societies, the ritual sacrifice would be staged in the format of a duel between the old king and his younger rival; the outcome was predetermined by administering drugs and alcohol to the intended loser, thus assuring his defeat and death. This spectacle also dramatically illustrated the cycle of life and death.)

In classical Greece and Rome, sexual activity was cherished and celebrated as a divine gift, with procreation viewed as only an incidental, and comparatively minor, corollary purpose to sexual indulgence. In both Greece and Rome, monogamy was not required of people as part of maintaining one's image as a good spouse or citizen, especially for men. Marriage was merely an institution with social and political implications, with only marginal relevance to one's choice of sexual partners. In addition, there were no social restrictions attached to sexual activity with either gender; bisexuality was common and accepted, and for men of that time young boys were at least as desirable sexual partners as young maidens.

Homer wrote at length, in both *The Iliad* and *The Odyssey*, about the virtues associated with a "good wife" in classical cultures. One of the most important qualities such a wife could display in demonstrating her loyalty and fidelity to her husband was the willingness to take in and raise children resulting from the sexual liaisons between her husband and other women as if they were her own issue.

Religious rituals celebrated sexuality, and the gods were portrayed as being every bit as sexually active and polygamous as any human. Indeed, children of dubious or contested paternity were simply categorized as children of a god, usually Zeus, and a mortal mother. Some—like Achilles and Aeneas—were believed to be the issue of a union between a mortal man and a goddess.

One god, Pan, was depicted with goat's horns protruding from his head as well as goat's legs, and often with an obviously erect penis. His followers would conclude festivals in his honor with sexual orgies which were held out in nature, and lasted for several days. Not surprisingly, in the sexually repressive early Christian religion Pan's image was adopted as the prototype for Satan, the source and agent of all evil. It was just such an orgiastic pagan festival that provided Shakespeare with the inspiration and setting for *A Midsummer Night's Dream*, though Shakespeare significantly modified the overt sexual content of the occasion so as not to offend the moral sensibilities of his Elizabethan audiences.

Temples in classical antiquity were often tended by a host of priestesses, among whose official functions was the extending of hospitality towards important visitors by making themselves sexually available to these guests of the state. Such women were viewed as "holy prostitutes," since both the extending of hospitality and sexuality were highly prized virtues in classical societies. These women enjoyed very high social status and privileges, and it was considered the ultimate good fortune for a prominent citizen to be able to entice one of them away from her religious functions and into matrimony. What's more, such women were still considered virgins while they serviced the guests of the city and the deity they served, regardless of the number of lovers they may have had in the course of fulfilling their duties at the temple. The perception of virginity coupled with considerable sexual experience and sophistication, rather than presenting a confusing apparent contradiction, added to their social desirability as wives to important men. The most prominent example of such an order of prostitute-priestesses recorded in history were the Vestal Virgins of Rome.

In prehistoric Britain, the Druids and Celts celebrated the advent of spring with bonfires and festivals which culminated in the mating of the tribe's women with the Great Horned God, embodied by the tribe's young men wearing the skin of a stag's head as a hood, complete with antlers. Children resulting from this orgiastic ritual were highly prized as divinely conceived beings, and were the collective responsibility of everyone within the tribe, with the identity of their mortal father never raised as an issue. In the legend of King Arthur, it was during such a ritual that Arthur fathered a son by his half-sister, Morganna LeFay. The son, Mordred, eventually revolted against his father in a war that culminated with a battle which was fatal to both father and son—as well as to most of the Knights of the Round Table, effectively dissolving the Order.

In our times, there is great cultural diversity with regard to sexual mores, and what is regarded as deviant in one culture is acceptable in another. Diverse sexual practices and mores seem to cause no emotional illness or destructive behavior, except in their repression and public censuring. For example, among many American Indian tribes homosexuality was honored and homosexuals regarded as special, with no negative connotation attached to that term.

Among certain tribes in Polynesia there is no institution of marriage or requirement for monogamy. Women are sexually active with as many men as they desire, and the resulting children are raised by the women and their brother(s), who assume the male supervisory role assigned to husbands in our culture. In yet another part of Polynesia, a girl's introduction to adulthood and sexuality occurs with her first act of intercourse in public, with one of her mother's brothers performing the initiation. This is followed by a feast, celebrating the young woman's entering into adult sexual activity and childbearing. In our culture, such an act would be considered incest and sexual abuse—not to mention the criticism that would attend *any* sexual act in public!

By contrast, several African tribes initiate their women sexually with a painful clitorectomy, surgical removal of the clitoris, because it is not considered "proper" for women to experience pleasure in the act of intercourse. This practice may seem barbaric, but is motivated by attitudes not very different from the Victorian tradition in our own culture, which considers any interest in sex or sexual pleasure expressed by women to be a sign of moral defect or psychopathology.

Women in Victorian England, as well as among more conservative American communities, have been taught to consider sex outside of marriage as a sin, and a wife's duty but not a source of pleasure for "proper" women within marriage. It is said that mothers in Victorian England instructed their about-to-be-wed daughters to submit to their husband's sexual advances, and to "lean back and think of England" during the sexual act itself. During this era, Sigmund Freud wrote that he considered women who experienced pleasure in the act of intercourse and who had orgasms as a result of clitoral stimulation as "neurotic."

One of the most outrageous and hypocritical features of western sexual "morality," and probably the single most important factor in creating dissonance between the genders is the so-called "double standard," which holds one level of interest and activity in sexual matters as acceptable or "natural" for men, but improper or promiscuous for women. In fact, the majority of terms implying negative judgment of sexual interest or conduct are applied to women. Of course, this double standard extends far beyond sexuality, into such matters as career options, salary levels, and child-rearing responsibilities. The sexual double standard dates back at least to the classical cultures mentioned earlier, and is only in our own time beginning to be scrutinized critically, but not yet lifted. According to this "double standard," it is at least understandable and acceptable for men to take an interest in sex and related matters, such as nudity, pornography, and erotic art; it is quite another matter when women express such interests. Out of a trepidation towards female sexuality that seems incomprehensible to emotionally healthy people of both genders, the traditional social standard for women is to expect them to avoid sexual matters and to be—at least publicly—shocked and embarrassed by them. According to this view, sex is something that men pursue, but that only happens to women at men's discretion. Moreover, monogamy is a strict expectation for "decent" women, but when men stray sexually from a committed relationship, the practice is usually winked at and dismissed with a "boys will be boys" casualness. The exception to this rule is the public highlighting of sexual indiscretions attributed to public figures, such as political candidates, supposedly as an indication of their defects of character.

In the same vein, extensive previous sexual experience is considered an asset in men when one is considering prospective sexual partners, but a liability in women. While virginity is no longer a common expectation for women entering a marital relationship, thanks to the "sexual revolution" of the 1960's, it is still considered desirable by many men in our culture to choose women with limited sexual experience and a small number of previous sexual partners when entering a committed relationship. Is this because of males' insecurity about their sexual performance, and their dread of any comparisons between them and any other lovers their woman may have had? If so, that may be also why the Victorians, the conservative Christians, the Moslems and the Freudians, just to name a few, discourage the active participation in and enjoyment of sex in women.

Louise Hay relates in one of her audio tapes that, thanks to her early religious training, she grew up believing that there was a deity sitting on a cloud somewhere who had nothing better to do than observe her attention to and use of her genitals, recording it all down to be used against her at her "final judgment!" Of course, she visualized this deity as an old man in a long white robe, with a flowing beard.

Modern psychiatry has further contributed to the conflict, stress and confusion around female sexuality by introducing terms and concepts which describe sexual dysfunction, such as "frigidity" and "nymphomania." These are applied to "abnormal" sexual interest and activity levels in women, not men. The only commonly used psychiatric label for male sexual dysfunction is "impotence"—a term applied to function, not level of desire. The implication is that whatever level of sexual desire men experience is okay, but the proper level of sexual desire in a woman is one directly correlated to that of her man. This suggests that a woman owes her identity, self-worth and perspective on life, including healthy sexuality, to her relationship with a man. She is intended to exist as an extension of a man, not as an independent person with her distinct and separate value. This includes exhibiting a level of sexual desire that exactly matches her man's, and includes never expressing dissatisfaction with the level of sexual demands—or lack of them—placed on her. "Too much" sexual interest—nymphomania—or "too little"—frigidity—makes her "abnormal!"

Healthy women must be encouraged to express their sexual feelings, and to expect their partners to have equal respect for their expectations, if truly healthy relationships are to occur. Indeed, that type of dialogue and equal exchange is an essential feature of any healthy relationship! Many of my female clients have enjoyed my definition of the term "bitch," and some have subsequently adopted it in describing themselves: "bitch" is an insecure male's term for a healthy woman who insists on having her needs met—in or out of the bedroom!

In this regard, it would help considerably if we could stop objectifying sexuality, as well as our sexual partners, thus somehow separating them from ourselves and our experience. In American society, women in particular are treated as objects, with their sexuality and desirability often described and exhibited separately from their person and all too often simply in terms of their body parts. For decades, American society has used the female body in various stages of nudity in advertising to sell cigarettes, automobiles, alcoholic beverages, and a wide variety of other items. Calendars and posters with virtually nude women are standard equipment in such male bastions as auto repair shops and construction site trailers. The culmination of this exploitation of the female body, accelerated by publications like *Playboy*, has been the "hard-core" video pornography that became widespread in the late 1960's and early '70's, and continues to grow in popularity. It is estimated that Americans spent in excess of $8 billion on pornography in

1996—an amount that dwarfs the total earnings of Hollywood's box office receipts and those of rock and country music recordings *combined*. The sudden, phenomenal popularity of pornography and of such establishments as "modeling studios" and topless bars indicate the degree to which males in our society have become comfortable in relating to women sexually in the most impersonal manner possible. It is not surprising that such "sexually oriented" businesses are most frequently encountered in the segment of the country where open and healthy human sexuality is most stigmatized, restricted and repressed—the area across the South known as "the Bible belt." Dallas, Texas, sometimes referred to as "the buckle on the Bible belt" and one of the most politically conservative cities in the nation, has the greatest concentration of topless bars of any urban area in the United States.

Can you envision any place in which healthy intimate contact between two people is less likely to occur than in a topless bar? Or any place where the men and women involved are less likely to get to know and appreciate each other as persons? The corresponding trend towards providing similar establishments and publications, in which women may view male bodies in various stages of undress has not provided equality—merely equal opportunity for objectifying and depersonalizing the other gender. This has only served to further widen the gap in intimacy between the genders.

With such diverse—and perverse!—expectations between men and women when it comes to sexuality, is it any wonder that there is so much confusion, insecurity, dissatisfaction, and resentment in the relations between the genders? It is time that we completely dispensed with the double standard of sexual mores and expectations that holds back *both* men and women in their relations to one another, and accepted their sexuality and sexual desire as gifts to be enjoyed by all in the course of human experience. Similarly, our hypocritical repression and condemnation of our bisexual and homosexual brothers and sisters needs to stop in a society claiming to be "enlightened" and "civilized!" One's sexuality, and sexual orientation, are as much a part of one's nature as hair color or height. We need to stop trying to impose different and unrealistic standards for different genders and sexual orientations, and accept everyone for who they are and what their nature attracts them towards, with the obvious exception of those who use sex in an abusive or hurtful manner.

Psychotherapists have come to recognize that acts such as rape or molestation are inspired by feelings of aggression, hostility and rage—not sexual desire. Those who would insist on labeling gay and lesbian people as "perverted" may do well to remember that true "perverts," such as rapists, child molesters and others who use sex as a weapon to hurt others, are overwhelmingly heterosexual.

We need to realize that there are no "good" or "bad" lovers, just as there are no "proper" or "unacceptable" sexual practices. One's experience of another as a "good" or "bad" lover has to do more with compatibility than with technique and frequency. For example, to someone with a low sexual appetite, someone who wants to make love three times a day will not be experienced as a good lover, but as an excessively demanding one. Everyone has a different level of sexual interest, and likes different practices and acts, much as various people have a preference for different foods or beverages. What we need in developing a healthy sexuality is acceptance of and compassion for one another. This includes compassion for all the inaccurate and destructive beliefs about gender and sexual orientation differences that our society has instilled in most of us from childhood, which keep us separate and interfere with our capacity to connect intimately with each other, sexually and otherwise. The concept can be applied among genders, as well as among people of various sexual orientations. Only when we are free to express and accept what each of us desires will we all be free to declare ourselves and be allowed to pursue and completely enjoy our desires, free of inhibitions or restrictions. That's not such a bad formula for all of human experience, not just sexuality.

At its best, healthy and enjoyable sexuality is carefree, playful and uninhibited. It is mutually satisfying, and respectful of both partners' desires, wants and inclinations, while also respecting each person's boundaries and turn-offs. Sexual pleasure and fulfillment goes considerably beyond orgasm, and has little relation to frequency, number of partners, variations of conventional and exotic positions, and other such standards by which compulsive people rate their performance and attractiveness. It is possible to experience impersonal sex, resentful sex, abusive sex and even boring sex. (Regrettably, for too many people, that last one is *not* an oxymoron!) Sex at its blissful best is not something you have, it is a process and an experience greater than oneself that takes you over. It is exhilarating, uplifting, and, along with meditation, the best way to get beyond one's physical limits and to the expansion into awareness of the greater Presence flowing through all of us. This may explain why young people having their first experiences of sex become so swept up by them and act as if they invented sex! Sexual connection to another and synergy with another may be felt without a stitch of clothing being removed, and without even touching. Sexual pleasure and bliss are not about intensity and frantic activity; they are about connection, intimacy, gratitude and appreciation. When the emphasis shifts from performance to relaxation and enjoyment, sex becomes blissful and fulfilling, and is truly lovemaking—expressing love of yourself, as well as your partner. That kind of lovemaking is like being in the home of your best friend, feeling wanted, welcome, nurtured and fulfilled. Lust comes from desiring a person's body, and wanting to use that body for your physical pleasure; true eroticism is about wanting to be with a person, and allowing your physical beings to express that connection to others. You can often hear the difference in perspective from people who talk about making love *to* someone rather than making love *with* someone. We're talking about more than just semantics here. The bottom line is that true intimacy and connection with another involves first being in touch with yourself and your own desires. In sex, this means being aware of your sexual feelings, and being able to openly communicate them to another. That's a level of interpersonal connection which is not encouraged in our culture. Open and healthy sexual expression has been suppressed for several centuries now in Western society. That may be because people who are that much in touch with themselves and their feelings, and so open about expressing them, listen and respond to their desires rather than others' expectations and limitations, in sexual as well as other matters.

Society tends to label such people as "dangerous," "antisocial" or "insane," because they are difficult to control and fit into social pigeonholes. There is also an implied message that to adopt such a perspective is to invite insanity and punishment in your life, which is why so many people are so inhibited about giving full expression to their true selves, sexual or otherwise. The result is that those who do allow themselves free sexual expression are often labeled as "dirty," or "immoral." Some are even regarded as "unnatural," if their modes of sexual expression are unfamiliar or uncomfortable for that someone else who is doing the judging.

If you are confused about your sexuality, here's a simple guide to clear your confusion: there's nothing about sex, about fantasy, or about dirt itself for that matter, that is "dirty." The application of that term simply imposes judgment, guilt and inhibition on its targets. Similarly, there is nothing immoral or unnatural about sex, with the obvious exception of acts that injure or otherwise violate another person. What is "natural" in sex is what feels good to you; anything that feels uncomfortable is not. After all, nobody has to tell you what you like or to whom you're attracted, do they? Sexuality is so central to our entire being, that its nature and expressions are as much a part of our overall makeup as our personality, intelligence and temperament. However, just like with different foods and types of music, you may have to expose yourself to a variety of sexual practices and situations before you discover and confirm your particular preferences. There's nothing wrong or unhealthy about such experimentation.

Sex is a very important part of healthy human experience, but it isn't serious. A serious attitude and good sex don't mix, any more than do comparative assessments of performance, number of lovers, etc. Sex at its best is playful and fun, and connects us to our creativity and godlike nature more than any other activity, while also helping us transcend the limits of our human experience, if only temporarily. This may be why so many invoke God in moments of sexual ecstasy, regardless of religious beliefs or affiliation. It returns us to the openness and freedom we enjoyed as children, before socialization intruded with what Albert Ellis refers to as "the tyranny of the shoulds." The greater connection to spirit that it gives us, as well as the increased connection and intimacy between two people, bring us closer to awareness of our eternal being than any experience except birth and death.

The emotional intensity of sex causes a lot of inhibited people to avoid openly discussing it, and encourages using clinical terms and euphemisms to refer to sexual organs and activities. These self-imposed limitations frequently cause decreases in experiences and enjoyment, as well. Good experiences with sex are available to everyone, at any time, regardless of how "good," "attractive," or even "sexy" they think they are. This is difficult for the individual ego to accept and allow, not to mention the greater societal ego. People read sex manuals, go to sex therapists, and pay thousands of dollars to attend seminars and workshops to "learn" how to be satisfied in this most basic, unstructured and natural of human activities. If you are affected by a sexual dysfunction of some kind, be it impotence, frigidity or whatever, don't spend thousands of dollars on someone or some technique that will help you "cure" or "overcome" it. Simply pay attention to its message about your relationship with your sexual self, and it will dissolve by itself, quickly and easily. Good, healthy sex is our birthright, our nature, and our vehicle of transcending ourselves and expressing our intimacy and connection to one another. Enjoy it, and help others you care about enjoy it with you!

Chapter 9

Addictions

The discussion of addictions deserves a separate section, although I plan to address their treatment also in the next chapter, devoted to mental health and psychotherapy. Addictions and the addictive process are so misunderstood, and their treatment so distorted and often rendered ineffectual by the medical model and its self-serving manipulation of 12-step programs, that an exposition of addictive processes and dynamics as well as effective treatments must be discussed at length and in detail. Such revelations and insights are not exposed here for the first time; many responsible professionals are already aware of these principles, and are effectively applying them with very encouraging and, for their clients, empowering results. However, the medically oriented establishment resists many of these methods, and suppresses the resulting encouraging findings, for a variety of reasons. Unfortunately, most of these reasons are motivated by self-serving views, and often ignore the best interests of their clients. This is often done with the acquiescence and compliance of many "12-steppers," who in conjunction with the medical establishment rigidly apply the principles of their program. Many devotees of 12-step groups have, in many respects, formed an alternative quasi-religion or cult out of what was originally intended to be a self-help program.

What are addictions? Carol Bridges, in her terrific and inspiring book, *The Medicine Woman's Guide to Being in Business for Yourself*, tells us that they are "sustained impulses of creative expression that have turned off on a tangent away from such expressive manifestations." The more deeply one is addicted, the more intense is that person's creative and spiritual nature, as well as his or her creative impulses. Addicts crave a transcendent experience which their creativity can provide, but usually distort it in the practice of their addiction, thus deriving great intensity from the experience, but at far less than the full range of their creative abilities. It is also true that there is only one basic addiction: the addictive impulse in human nature to numb uncomfortable feelings and redirect creative impulses, lest we be held responsible for learning from or implementing them in our lives. Instead, many addicts seem to choose instead an alternative drive, to maintain a level of contentment with a meager existence. This sustained low level of existence and achievement is maintained by indulgence in the addiction.

Unfortunately, for some recovering addicts, it is also maintained by excessive involvement in recovery groups and activities.

It may be a part of human nature to avoid risking disappointment and the label of "failure;" or, this may be a conditioned response in a culture which discourages individualism and creativity by preaching the virtues of conformity, and discounting the worth of the person. The many behavioral and chemical manifestations of this addictive impulse serve the inclination to avoid stress and numb oneself. When no healthy alternative is perceived, it is common to see addicts abandon the diminishing satisfaction of one addictive behavior for the novelty of another, which also wears thin in time.

It is this capacity for being able to readily substitute one form of addiction for another, and the fact that it is the rare addict who confines him/herself to one form of addictive indulgence, that has brought me to come to the understanding that there is only one addiction. This is the compulsive urge to gain pleasure while suppressing feelings and arousing guilt that has varied possible outlets for most addicts. You can readily observe a demonstration of this substitution of one form of addiction for another by attending any meeting of Alcoholics Anonymous, or Narcotics Anonymous: most participants will be greedily indulging alternative addictive impulses to nicotine, caffeine and sugar during breaks, all the while lauding their "recovery" from the highlighted addiction. Robin Williams likes to tell of his mother's habitual daily consumption of 10 cigarettes and 8 cups of coffee before 8 a.m., all the while proclaiming, "your father and I never did drugs!"

So many fantastically gifted and talented people throughout history have also been addicts, reaffirming the interrelationship between creativity and the addictive impulse: Alexander the Great, King Richard the Lionhearted, Edgar Allan Poe, Jack London, Ernest Hemingway, and Spencer Tracy were alcoholics; Samuel Coleridge, Vincent van Gogh, Sigmund Freud, and Judy Garland were addicted to drugs; Fyodor Dostoevsky was a compulsive gambler; St. Augustine, Shakespeare and Lord Byron were compulsive sex addicts. Closer to our time, we have the seemingly endless womanizing of John Kennedy, Marilyn Monroe's dependence on both drugs and alcohol at the expense of any fulfilling personal life, the compulsive overeating of "Mama" Cass Elliott, Janis Joplin's and Jimi Hendrix's fatal bouts with drugs, Karen Carpenter's fatal anorexia, Eric Clapton's recovery from a heroin habit, Richard Pryor's self-immolation from freebasing cocaine, and John Belushi's death from a drug-and-alcohol overdose. This list is by no means all-inclusive; a comprehensive listing of famous addicts, even one confined to those in my generation, would require a separate and very large volume. This abbreviated listing is merely offered here to illustrate that, while its forms of expression may have changed and evolved, addiction is as old as the human race, and has been a significant factor in all of human history. Each of the people named above exhibited talents far greater than most ordinary people; and, each became as well-known for his/her addictive indulgences as for creative genius.

It is easy to see the correlation between creative capacity and addiction when one looks at historical figures who have displayed ample evidence of both. But what about the ordinary "man on the street?" Estimates of the proliferation of addiction in our society indicate that it manifests among us in epidemic proportions. It is estimated that one out of eight Americans is an alcoholic; and alcoholism is but one facet of the addictive prism. We also have over 50 million cigarette smokers, in the face of decades of conclusive evidence about the extensive damage perpetrated by tobacco smoke on the human body. Millions are addicted to a variety of drugs, both illegal "street drugs" and prescription medications. Compulsive gamblers support the legal casinos in Las Vegas, Atlantic City and on Indian reservations; they also spend billions annually in state lotteries and in betting on sports events from the Super Bowl to the local high school basketball game. Workaholics, perhaps the addicts most supported by a results and achievement oriented culture, build careers, businesses and bank accounts at the expense of personal relationships and family life. There are also religious fanatics, people who spend their days attending numerous daily 12-step meetings, or watching soap operas and inane talk shows on television, and who knows what else.

When you consider all the possibilities, it's easier to exclude the small minority seemingly unaffected by the many manifestations of addiction than to count and catalogue the overwhelming majority affected by one phase of addiction or another. Well, does that mean that there are so many creative people around us who are using addictive behaviors to stifle or contain their creativity? The answer is a resounding "yes," and the implications of that realization are both encouraging and distressing.

As we already mentioned in the chapter on work and vocations, most people do what they perceive that they have to do to make a living, to get by from day to day and week to week, rather than fulfilling their purpose in life in a manner that rewards them spiritually and emotionally, as well as financially. By choosing jobs and careers for their immediate financial return, rather than following the calling of their spiritual and creative nature, they lock themselves into vocational monetary traps. Such jobs become manifestations of their perceived limitations, rather than expressions of their aspirations. The same is true of choices in personal relationships: people who enter personal relationships for reasons other than love, and who stay in them because of guilt or a misplaced sense of duty, must cope with and compensate for their sustained disappointment and lack of fulfillment in other ways. One of the ways to do so—and apparently the most popular one in our society—is to deaden their uncomfortable feelings by indulging in addictive behaviors. People become chronic drinkers, drug addicts, smokers, or overworkers, and use the addiction as an attempt to compensate for the good feelings they've missed out on by being in unsatisfying situations. Moreover, the very existence of such circumstances in their lives reinforce the suspicion that they are somehow destined to settle for less than they aspire to, which supports their self-image as flawed and inadequate beings. This self-perception invites feelings of shame about who they are, as well as about the direction of their lives, allowing them to consider seeking pleasure in activities that they also consider shameful. As any professional working in the field of addictions will tell you, the intertwining of impersonal pleasure seeking with feelings of shame about the process is the cyclical dynamic—the "catch-22"—at the center of the addictive process.

If you ever wish to observe the manifestation of this process—the stressful and unsatisfying lifestyle, with the corresponding indulgence in addictive behaviors in order to compensate—just go to any bar or pub during Friday's "happy hour," in an area of town where there is a high concentration of high-stress jobs, such as the financial center or the courthouse. You will observe crowds of people using alcohol, cigarettes and the pursuit of casual sex to numb themselves, and to seek some temporary relief from their life's pressures. When left unchecked, this process becomes an overwhelming obsession of its own that can lead to the destruction of the individual.

Two excellent fictional works, both of which have been made into movies, depict this process very poignantly: *The Days of Wine and Roses*, and *Looking for Mr. Goodbar*, which was based on a real-life murder case in New York City.

The ever-increasing consumption of cigarettes, alcohol and drugs in spite of scientific evidence graphically demonstrating the destructive effects of their use indicates the level of dissatisfaction with life in our society, and the desire of people to even temporarily escape their emotional pain, even at the expense of their health. That is the distressing realization to be derived from the statistics showing the proliferation of addiction; the encouraging "flip side" of this coin is that there is this much creative energy among us, even if so much of it is currently subverted into addiction and mostly stifled by our limiting beliefs and confining social institutions. It is uplifting to realize that those beliefs and institutions can be changed. Our perception of their validity and permanence is *all* that gives them their permanent appearance; and this can be changed in the blink of an eye, if we are willing to change it! If enough people are willing to make such changes in their life, to live their life pursuing their dreams and desires rather than confining themselves according to outdated and dysfunctional institutionalized beliefs, the release of creative energy and happiness resulting will make this the happiest and liveliest planet in the universe. Don't be fooled in this regard by the negative assertions of traditionalists and pessimists. The shift in consciousness that can and will produce this dramatic shift in the nature of human experience is coming like a giant tidal wave!

Let's backtrack just a bit and see how we got stuck in the reliance on addictions to temporarily relieve our uncomfortable feelings, and to use the proliferation of addictions to maintain society's dysfunctional traditions. As we noted earlier, addictions have been with us throughout history:

In ancient Sparta, there was one day per year when the citizens would force their slaves to get drunk, and then parade them through the streets as a warning to the young about the trappings of overindulgence.

In classical Rome, there was a custom of holding banquets and orgies that lasted for days, with houses having large cisterns into which the celebrants could intentionally vomit so they might further indulge in eating and drinking. The Roman predilection for hedonistic overindulgences also gave us the cliche' "Roman orgy," which requires no further explanation here.

The earliest Moslem invaders would use hashish to alleviate their soldiers' fears before entering battle, so they would be more reckless in attacking the enemy. These soldiers were called "hashishin," and from that term is derived our word "assassin."

Throughout history, societies have publicly condemned addictive behaviors and patterns while covertly encouraging them, so as to keep their citizens sufficiently numbed in order to maintain their compliance with the desires and initiatives of the ruling class. In the industrialized western world, people were—and still are—expected to train, marry, fulfill traditional roles in both the workplace and at home, and to act satisfied with their lot in life while awaiting their greater reward for their life's struggle in heaven. Changing careers is often condemned as "irresponsible," changing mates is still stigmatized in many circles, and changing life perspectives and direction is generally frowned upon unless it has obvious and immediate value for society as a whole, according to its standards. From society's prevailing view, it is irresponsible to leave a corporate position in New York City to go be a sculptor in Taos, New Mexico, but a sign of social responsibility, an indication of coming to one's senses and being willing to become a productive member of society, to do the reverse. In such a social climate, addictions are still publicly condemned but covertly encouraged as an effective means to stifle creativity and original thought, while providing just enough temporary relief to keep the individual stuck in place. This fulfills society's needs, and simplifies the bookkeeping, by securing the performance of necessary functions while also making it easy to keep track of who's living with whom, who's responsible for supporting which children, who owes how much tax, and so on.

The extent to which people depend on addictive behaviors to maintain themselves in an otherwise unsatisfying existence may not be fully appreciated. We've already referred to the proliferation of smoking, especially among the very young, in the face of massive and conclusive evidence regarding the health hazards involved. We also have the example of Prohibition earlier in our century, during which alcohol consumption barely slowed down even though drinking was made illegal. More recently, attempts to ban gambling have given way to state-sanctioned gambling networks, including off-track betting, state lotteries, and a proliferation of casinos in 28 of the 50 states, as of this writing. Several American Indian tribes, encouraged by their tax-exempt status, have come to rely on casinos within their reservations for a substantial portion of their income. (One tribal spokesman referred to casino gambling as "the new buffalo" on which the tribes' livelihood depends.) The cost of addictions due to such proliferation, however, has exceeded their value as social palliatives in most cases. Has anyone noticed a significant improvement on the overall quality of education in the many states which have instituted state lotteries, with the additional funds supposedly earmarked for improving our schools?

The response of the medical establishment has been to provide forms of treatment and aftercare which all too often substitute one form of addiction for another. Detoxification in a setting restricted from the "problem" substance in question is routinely followed by substitution for that substance with prescription medications, presumably with the intent to calm down the person sufficiently and ease withdrawal symptoms.

In practice, what actually occurs in all too many cases is a long-term dependency on these new drugs, which can prove just as debilitating to the patient in the long run as the original addiction. In fact, the addict's inclination towards denial of the seriousness of his dependency is aided by this trade-off, as is our collective denial. Prescription drugs, since they are dispensed legally and through the intervention of a doctor, are not recognized by many as possible problematic and addictive substances; that designation is reserved for the illegal "street drugs" dispensed by criminals. Yet prescription drugs are themselves a major area of concern, because of the excessive commonality of their use which is facilitated by the lack of social stigma attached to them. Well-meaning doctors, as well as less ethical and more mercenary ones who don't mind encouraging long-term dependency in their clients, dispense such drugs a bit too freely in order to help their patients feel better and be more comfortable. When lives are shortened or ruined by such drugs, it is easy to overlook the role of legally dispensed addictive substances in the tragedy; after all, excessive reliance on prescribed drugs is not considered by many to be addiction, but rather "treatment." The only time such misuse of prescription drugs is noticed is in cases where they may obviously be connected to the tragic results, as was the case with the death of Elvis Presley.

Doctors themselves have an unusually high incidence of drug addiction, due to the demanding nature of their work combined with many doctors' perceived need to maintain a more-than-human image. These factors often prevent them from seeking treatment for their addictions, as well. Moreover, doctors have easy access to legal drugs, and benefit from the reluctance of most health professionals to question a doctor's decisions, or "blow the whistle" on a colleague.

The traditional model of recovery most widely used in treatment facilities today, based on the medical perspective combined with the 12-step program of Alcoholics Anonymous, also presents some important problems and questions (some procedural, others ethical) in the aftercare process. According to this model, "once an addict, always an addict." An addicted person may enter a recovery process, but this process is presented as a lifelong commitment—and identity—for him or her, demanding continuous participation, but failing to ever reach completion. This means that the person is locked in with the addiction for life, forever fluctuating between two stages: recovery or relapse. The substance(s) and/or behavior(s) associated with the addiction can never be indulged in again, even in moderation. The exceptions to this are, of course, addictions involving the misuse of food and sex. Since these two are necessary and natural functions essential for healthy lifestyles and relationships, modification of behaviors rather than total abstinence is the goal. This raises the question that, if modification rather than abstinence works with these addictions, *why not with all the others?*

One of the generally acknowledged characteristics of an addict is the inclination towards all-or-nothing, or "black-and-white" thinking in 12-step parlance, with no moderate alternatives or middle-ground choices considered or acknowledged. Ironically, the very same traditionally-oriented professionals and institutions which profess as their goal aiding the addict in entering and maintaining recovery—including the personality characteristics which make the onset and occurrence of addictive behaviors more likely—exhibit the same all-or-nothing mentality in outlining the conditions of recovery which they identify in the addict as descriptive of the disease! In addition, the emotional burden of never being able to shed the stigmatizing label of addiction, since one is always "recovering" but never completely "recovered," causes diminished self-esteem in the person. This medical "mark of Cain" becomes in itself a liability in precipitating future relapse by ensuring that the person remains in a state of lowered self-esteem by virtue of being forever saddled with this addictive identity. Yet, this perpetual stigmatization is precisely what is encouraged by the medical establishment and its 12-step supporters, many of whom see in this perspective the opportunity for exploiting for greater profit the lifetime allegiance and dependency of their patients. This is because such a perspective presents opportunities for perpetual psychotherapy and inpatient treatment with these same patients when relapse, or the mere threat of it, occurs.

Equally distorting and damaging is the influence of the addiction diagnosis on future psychological and spiritual issues arising in the client's life; all future issues and problems are from then on viewed and treated in relation to the addiction, thus making it a central factor in any and all pathology that might ever arise. This keeps the client focused on the addiction to the virtual exclusion of other life issues; and it ensures that in most cases the other personal problems that might occur are never fully appreciated and treated on their own merit and gravity, but rather as symptoms associated with and resulting from the addictive process.

Just as important and potentially damaging as the perpetual labeling and fostered dependency of clients is the focus of medical and 12-step groups on the substance(s) or behavior(s) on which the addict is focused. This means that alcoholics are strongly encouraged to abstain from drinking, and drug addicts from using drugs; but what is nominally addressed, if at all, is the emotional and mental disturbance that created the opportunity for the addiction to manifest in the first place. Similarly, although 12-step programs profess a strong reliance on spirituality in their programs, the counterproductive emphasis on a "higher power" *outside* the person (be that higher power God, AA itself, or one's recovery group) keeps this concept as mystifying, inaccessible, and useless for most clients as the mysterious and nebulous constructs of most organized religions. It is this emphasis on an external higher power which provides long-term relief from the manifestation of the addictive behavior at the expense of forfeiting an opportunity for final resolution, which can only come from *within* the person, where the source of our connection to the divine is located as well. How much more effective, empowering, and healing would 12-step programs be if they directed their adherents to the infinite, divinely provided healing power that lies within all of us instead!

Although the opportunity is there, far too few participants in 12-step programs take advantage of the full opportunity to really work all of the steps, thereby developing a really intimate bond with their spiritual nature and reaching the level of self-forgiveness and resolution necessary to complete the recovery process. Perhaps this is because even veteran participants and sponsors within such groups lack the sophistication and determination to guide themselves and others through such a depth of self-exploration, and may be a great part of the reason for the widely accepted estimate that only one of thirty persons in 12-step groups is able to maintain long-term recovery. Since true recovery involves a recovery of the sense of one's innate spiritual basis, the grim long-term statistics of addiction are not surprising.

It is also possible that the very concept of a lifelong process of recovery seems overwhelming for many people, possibly because it never offers the prospect of completion. Whatever the reasons, the vast majority of 12-step adherents who are able to maintain recovery from indulgence in one substance or behavior become at least equally dependent on alternative substances, like cigarettes and coffee, or behaviors, like excessive group attendance or obsession with the recovery process. These new, compensatory dependencies are frequently just as effective in preventing a person's full participation in life and relationships as the original addiction. Most such people readily, perhaps reflexively, mouth platitudes such as "one day at a time," "let go and let God," etc., without fully appreciating the concepts and depth of meaning behind such slogans. Thus, 12-step adherents are often deprived of the opportunity to fully access the spiritual strength and fulfillment available to us all, and instead pay lip service to abstract concepts of "higher powers" which are external and consequently remain foreign to them, ensuring their lack of complete healing in the all-important spiritual area. The unfortunate consequence of incomplete spiritual healing is that it leaves many adherents of 12-step programs as "dry drunks," people who learn to stop drinking in recovery but never quite get in touch with their true nature, or recover their capacity for fulfilling relationships and a full life. In one extreme manifestation of such limited thinking, this condition causes excessive reliance on the recovery group. Many such people come to view attending groups as the focus of their total participation and the most meaningful interaction of their lives, often to the exclusion or in lieu of intimate personal relationships and friendships.

I cannot emphasize this point enough: as long as the center of healing and personal power is focused *outside* the person, what is called "recovery" must necessarily be a limited process that is woefully inadequate in helping the addict get past the addictive process and realize his full potential as a human being. It is only when the emphasis is on recovering one's awareness of the spirit within (the only true recovery worthy of the term) that the addict can dissolve the shame that is the basis of addiction, and realize the full wonder of everyone's true identity!

The shift that is necessary here is the change in perspective from focus on and stigmatization of addictive behaviors to the deeper emotional and spiritual issues which gave opportunity for the addiction to become established in the first place. We must come to recognize that addiction is much more than a medical disease; it is an important and very dangerous symptom of a much deeper emotional and/or spiritual wound in need of healing. As we will see before the conclusion of this section, it is also a dangerous illusion that can be lifted, freeing people to live fulfilling and guilt-free lives.

In colonial times, per capita consumption of alcohol was about six times higher than it is today. Yet, alcohol consumption was not condemned and fraught with shame, because liquor was not perceived as the catalyst through which people engaged in antisocial, self-destructive or criminal behaviors. In colonial times, the town pub was a gathering place for the entire family, a place where friends and neighbors met to commune with one another. Acquaintances were renewed, friendships cemented, and differences resolved. Children were included, and women were invited to participate in drinking, recreation and socializing as equals. It wasn't until the next century, when "temperance" and religious movements demonized the consumption of alcohol, that alcoholism became a recognized and widespread social disease, and became associated in the collective mind with corollary deviant and antisocial behaviors and traits.

In Europe, Mediterranean and eastern European cultures permit and invite alcohol consumption from an early age, as part of a person's socialization process. Children are routinely given wine and beer with meals; consumption of alcohol is at much greater levels than in American society, and is not considered deviant or otherwise stigmatized. These cultures have among the lowest rates of alcoholism in the civilized world, and—contrary to expectations from American health standards—boast some of the most remarkable longevity statistics anywhere on the globe. Societies such as those in the former Soviet republics of Georgia and Armenia routinely boast centenarians, and people stay not only alive, but active and productive well into their nineties and well beyond. This remarkable longevity is achieved in spite of drinking water glasses full of vodka daily, smoking, and consuming a high-fat diet. These examples demonstrate that it's not what you ingest that counts, but *how* (with what attitudes, motivations and expectations) you consume it. What is consumed with genuine pleasure increases pleasure in life and self-esteem; what is ingested in an atmosphere of stress and guilt causes dependency and results in disease.

There is considerable sentiment recently in support of legalizing all drugs. This initiative correlates with the legalization and expansion of state-supported gambling, as we have come to recognize that people inclined towards addictive behaviors will indulge those behaviors whether they risk coming into conflict with law enforcement agencies or not, and whether they compromise other aspects of their personal lives or not. We already mentioned that Prohibition had a negligible effect in reducing Americans' consumption of alcohol. The same can be said of money spent on gambling in America before and after widespread legalization. Our society is beginning to recognize the strong allure and permanence of such behaviors, and is adopting an "if you can't beat them, join them" attitude, which will probably expand to include drugs before long.

It is very distressing that social trends move towards acceptance and legalization of addictive behaviors, but so far stop short of the greater development that would remove the reasons for the very existence of addictions: the removal of the coercive and restrictive social institutions and conventions that motivate people to indulge in addictions in the first place. Releasing people from traditional standards of conduct, "morality," "responsibility," and "duty" in favor of allowing them to choose and alter their lifestyles in any way(s) desirable to them would release a level of creative energy and joy in life that would transform daily living into a state of bliss that is currently unimaginable.

As George Bernard Shaw noted in his classic work *Man and Superman*, it is the "seven deadly virtues" that are the cause of all the conflict and distress on earth, so it would be appropriate that their adherents would find the rewards for promoting and supporting them in Hell, a self-created hell into which they have voluntarily confined themselves. Dispensing with the "shoulds" imposed by society will afford everyone the freedom to live as they want, making escape through altered moods and self-medication, the primary results of addictive behaviors, unnecessary. This would open the way to self-expression, creativity, and a blissful and rewarding existence far beyond hedonism and self-indulgence.

Deepak Chopra writes in *Unconditional Life* that our brain has neuroreceptors which are receptive to drugs, alcohol and the body's own stimulants that are released with the excitation resulting from indulging behavioral addictions, such as compulsive sex or gambling. It is highly unlikely that these neuroreceptors would have evolved in our brain thousands of years before the availability of the substances themselves; what is more likely is that addictive substances correspond to pleasure-giving substances which the body itself is capable of producing, and which have always been available to us naturally. It is only when we lose sight of our capability to provide such pleasure-inducing substances to ourselves that we turn to external sources. In this insight lies the one permanent prospect for overcoming addiction and its corollary self-destructive behaviors.

Dr. Chopra relates a very effective treatment plan for addictions in this book, in a chapter appropriately titled *Paradise Remembered.* He examines the flawed cycle of addiction that combines the alternate pursuit of pleasure with the suffering of guilt, with neither feeling ever gathering enough strength to completely supplant the other and end the cycle. He also notes that a significant segment of people in our culture can never allow themselves to experience pleasure that is completely untainted by guilt, or without an accompanying feeling that some compensatory ill must always be paired with feelings of bliss. For some people, *any* feeling of pleasure is uncomfortable and shameful in and of itself, so that pleasure is perverted by being paired with dissatisfaction and shame. As some professionals in the addictions field like to observe, such people "can never get enough of what they don't want." Dr. Chopra notes that the circular pattern of pleasure and shame forms the core of the addict's compulsion, and is also the basis for his despairing assumption that he is incapable of self-healing, leading to his perpetual reliance on recovery groups and other external "higher powers." However, the Ayurvedic tradition of India maintains that human awareness is complete and all-powerful, and therefore capable of self-healing in any area, including addiction. Dr. Chopra describes the treatment plan that resolves the impasse of the addictive cycle, resulting from reliance on self-awareness.

Dr. Chopra writes: "Evelyn Silvers, a Los Angeles therapist who specializes in drug addiction, has learned to create a remarkable phenomenon with her patients that releases them from the bondage of their cravings. Using the simplest sort of suggestion and guided thinking, she induces her patients to manufacture 'brain drugs' that appear to act exactly like the heroin, alcohol, cocaine, or tranquilizers that they have been ruining their lives to buy or steal."

As Dr. Chopra further relates, in earlier work with patients suffering from chronic pain Ms. Silvers discovered that she could influence such patients to produce pain relievers within their brain on command. These naturally-produced pain relievers were discovered to be much more powerful than morphine or other opiates. Doctors were aware of the body's capability to produce its own pain relievers, because they were familiar with accounts of wounded soldiers and accident victims who did not experience any pain from serious injuries for long intervals. Ms. Silvers' breakthrough contribution was in her ability to train people to consciously produce these body chemicals at will.

Using visualization techniques, she had her clients imagine creating a supply of endorphins or painkillers within their heads, but to not release the drugs into their system until commanded to do so. When the command to release the drugs was finally given, the results were astounding! All the clients reported immediate pain relief and euphoria, comparable to patients being provided morphine through an IV. Clients sent home with instructions to use this "brain drug" technique on their own were able to do so effectively enough to wean themselves off prescribed pain killers. More importantly, chronic pain patients who were also drug addicts were able to use the technique to relieve themselves of all drug cravings along with the pain, and without suffering from withdrawal symptoms in the process!

Encouraged by these results, Ms. Silvers then decided to apply this technique in the treatment of drug addiction. Her initial group was composed of twenty "hard-core" addicts who admitted to from five to forty years of dependency on a variety of substances, including alcohol, cocaine, heroin and other drugs. They had not been able to stop abusing drugs through other interventions, and most experienced serious health problems which could be directly attributed to their years of chemical abuse. Most subjects also reported having ruined their family and professional lives due to their pursuit of their addictions.

Ms. Silvers instructed the subjects in the "brain drug" technique, but also told them that the brain is capable of producing the exact chemical counterpart of any street drug. Thus, the addicts could have a lifetime supply of their drug of choice, at no cost and with no side effects! She told her subjects, "You have been using drugs for a very good reason. The drugs that get abused are precisely those that mimic the natural substances which the brain uses to make people feel normal. When we say that we feel a certain way, our mood is always produced by one brain chemical or other—there is no state of mind without a biochemical foundation.

"In the brain of an addicted person, the internal drugs for feeling normal—happy, calm, balanced, and in control—are in short supply, either because of a hereditary or spontaneous shortage, or because taking outside drugs lowers the brain's ability to produce its own supply.

"Your addictive cravings have been telling you that your brain was having a problem, and your habit was a way of solving it. Although drug abuse has dangerous consequences, it is nothing to be ashamed of in itself. You were just medicating yourself, like a diabetic taking insulin."

Here, Dr. Chopra notes that Ms. Silvers went out on a medical limb of sorts, because there is no scientific evidence to demonstrate that the body can produce chemicals identical to some addictive drugs, such as alcohol, nicotine and cocaine. Still, the fact that our brains have neuroreceptors that respond to these drugs indicates that it is highly likely that the body can replicate these substances. In any case, Ms. Silvers' findings with these clients were nothing short of remarkable, and their importance is obvious.

Each of the clients visualized producing a large dose of the preferred substance, and released it on command. Each client then displayed symptoms and behaviors consistent with a strong "high" produced by their drug of choice. Alcoholics relaxed visibly, and spoke openly about threatening subjects. Valium addicts stuttered, and cocaine addicts reported a massive rush. The "highs" were so strong that it was twenty minutes before the group could recover sufficiently to report their experiences. Even those who had been skeptical at the beginning of the session had enjoyed a strong "high" consistent with their addiction.

Ms. Silvers had found a way to overcome the hold of addiction on these people by removing guilt from her subjects. As she told them, "For years, the drug has been in control of you; now it will be the other way around." The brain has no will of its own to either continue or overcome addiction. It can only respond to the mind's directives in choosing an alternative.

Ms. Silvers' results, remarkable as they are, cannot be explained in terms of known brain structures or chemistry. Even she freely admitted that her findings rely on a source and capability within the person that has not been identified. The explanation, then, must be at a different, higher level: Dr. Chopra's assertion that it must involve accessing a new level of awareness. He explains that the mind can and has transcended the body's chemical abilities, because the mind is infinitely capable and resourceful. Ms. Silvers offered the addicts a "high" unrelated to the ingesting of external drugs, thus unmasking addiction as an illusion supported by the addict's beliefs about its nature. As Dr. Chopra writes, "years of pain, frustration and demolished self-esteem were suddenly irrelevant" for her clients, contrary to what traditional recovery models might have led one to believe about the inescapability of their condition. By raising our awareness, and by employing it to recover our joyful divinity that is the basis of our natural being, we can dissolve any dependency or assumed "reality," including addiction.

Chapter 10

Modern Medical and
Mental Health Care

As we learned from the recent efforts by the Clinton administration to nationalize the health-care system, one-seventh of the nation's economy revolves around the medical and mental health professions. Medical care in America is big business, and many important and powerful interests are grabbing for a piece of the pie. It was never made clear whether the estimate of the economy's share devoted to health care included the financial interests of such corollary businesses as the insurance companies, chemical and drug manufacturers, malpractice lawyers and the funeral industry; if not, then the additional billions of dollars involved would really be mind-boggling.

Medicine has made greater advances in the last century than in all of previous history combined. The introduction of anaesthetic drugs has made extensive surgical procedures possible with a fraction of the discomfort and many times the precision possible in the past. Laser surgery and bloodless procedures have significantly increased surgical precision and possible interventions, while minimizing the invasive and damaging effects on the patient's body. Vital organs are now almost routinely transplanted, and microsurgery has made reattachment and resectioning possible, so that the body can now be repaired and replenished in ways that were unimaginable even a generation ago. Life expectancy has dramatically increased, to nearly double what it was a century ago. It seems destined to continue increasing at fantastic and heretofore unimagined rates.

Unfortunately, the technical and scientific advances in medicine are not always paralleled by similar advances in understanding and compassion in the way that most doctors perceive their patients, or design their treatment plans. Modern, scientifically-based medicine views the patient as a body to be worked *on*, not as a person to be worked *with*, in restoring the body to healthy functioning. Illness is viewed as the consequence of poorly functioning organs, chemical imbalances, and bodily processes gone awry. Consequently, medical treatment is designed to revolve around the dispensing of drugs, application of chemicals, and invasive (and potentially harmful) radiation and surgery. In an age of extreme specialization, many doctors prescribe treatment programs better suited to treatment by their area of expertise, than to the best interests of their patient, because maximizing the quality of patient care is all too often a secondary consideration to a doctor's earning potential. At a time when malpractice litigation is a real and frequent threat, patients' treatment is routinely continued and extended beyond optimal limits, so that if death occurs it will occur while treatment is still being administered, preventing lawsuits for inadequate care. To date, there have been no lawsuits that I'm aware of for *excessive* treatment, even if this is to the patient's detriment. Excessive treatment is often the case with cancer and AIDS patients, who are exposed to radiation, chemotherapy and other biochemical and surgical treatments long after recovery has become impossible—and the onset of death is often actually accelerated by such procedures, when they're applied to an already weakened organism.

Another factor contributing to inappropriate and/or excessive treatment of patients is that, in a time in which the cost of medical care has spiraled to dizzying heights, and the savings of a lifetime can easily evaporate in a month of inpatient medical treatment, a majority of patients must rely on insurance and government subsidies in order to pay for their care. With this ready alternative source of income available to them, many doctors are more willing than ever to expose their patients to excessive, unnecessary, and even dangerous procedures that may actually be dangerous for the patient, but enriching for the doctor. This is the real underlying motive behind many doctors' expressed zeal to combat and delay the onset of death "at any cost," even at the expense of the patient's comfort and dignity. Consider the following:

In my personal experience, I have witnessed doctors recommending to several of my AIDS patients' families invasive, expensive and uncomfortable "treatments," when it was clear that death at this point was not only imminent but desirable for the patient. These doctors played on the family's grief and guilt with pleas that "everything must be tried before we give up on him," in an obvious attempt to inflate the bill to the patient's insurance provider.

When my father, then almost 80 years old, was diagnosed with inoperable lung cancer and given no more than two months to live, a hospital surgeon who was not even assigned to treating him walked into his hospital room and offered to perform an operation on his cancer-riddled lungs. When I declined his offer because I recognized the futility of such a procedure and the unnecessary pain it would cause to my father, this doctor's immediate loss of interest in this case could not have been more obvious: he immediately turned on his heels and walked out. Several weeks after my father's death, my family received a bill from this doctor's office for a "consultation," in excess of $100. I remember taking great pleasure in shredding and disposing of the bill.

A woman whose presence in my life was very important (please refer to the acknowledgment at the beginning of this book) was diagnosed with cervical cancer, and underwent a complete hysterectomy followed by several months of radiation and chemotherapy. After it became apparent that these treatments were ineffective, and in fact were contributing more to the deterioration of her health than the cancer itself, her doctors recommended their "indefinite" continuation. Presumably this was so that she might at least die "in treatment," protecting them from possible litigation, as well as ensuring a continuation of billable hospital visits, at the expense of her life.

Keep in mind that procedures like radiation and chemotherapy are efforts to eradicate the malignancy before they kill the patient; but the procedures are equally and indiscriminately destructive to both healthy and malignant tissues, so it is never certain which will occur first. What *is* certain is that the doctor and the hospital will be reimbursed for the treatments, and neither can be subsequently sued by the patient's loved ones for not having done enough. Granted, the incidents recounted here are anecdotal; but twenty years of working within the medical establishment have convinced me that they are by no means atypical. Statistics compiled by insurance companies and government agencies bear this out: experts even more intimately acquainted than myself with the medical profession in America confirm the widespread abuses in the system. They estimate that as many as 80 percent of the hysterectomies performed in America may be unnecessary; radical mastectomies are performed in numbers way out of proportion to their

actual need; and hospitalized patients with insurance are unnecessarily exposed to harmful radiation by doctors ordering
excessive and repetitive, but insurance-compensated, X-rays far
beyond actual need. Many doctors respond to such charges
with assertions that they are the only ones with sufficient
expertise to decide which procedures are appropriate, and how
often, and that this assumed expertise renders them immune
to professional criticisms from outside the medical fraternity.
This arrogance is countered by more sober assessments from
both within and outside the profession, which confirm the
widespread excesses as well as the reluctance of most doctors
to effectively police their profession and expose their less-than-
ethical and profit-motivated colleagues. Insurance companies
have come to recognize these widespread excesses and abuses
in the dispensing of medical treatment; many have now responded to such practices by instituting a predetermined "cap"
on compensation for particular procedures, and try to avoid
paying for duplicate procedures by limiting length of care and
excluding payment for "pre-existing" (already treated) conditions. Unfortunately, such measures by the insurance companies limit some less fortunate patients from getting treatment
they need, more often than they effectively curb the doctors'
avarice.

There is ample reason for the public to be wary of the
medical profession and its motives, and to be aware that
monetary interests and political advantage often supersede any

concern with patients' care or the quality of public health. This is not only true of many individual doctors, but also of the political bulwark of the profession, the American Medical Association.

The AMA approves legislative and economic measures which effectively limit the numbers of practicing doctors, even though a significant percentage of the population has grossly inadequate medical care, in order to ensure that currently practicing doctors' income opportunities are not diminished by too many competitors. It delays and blocks distribution of potentially beneficial medication and alternative treatments in order to ensure maximum profits for the medical and pharmaceutical professions, in the process compromising many patients' quality of life, and causing many preventable relapses and deaths. (I saw repeated and tragic evidence of this policy and its effects during my work with AIDS patients.) And finally, it pursues politically advantageous alliances, often at the expense of the public it professes to serve. Perhaps the most graphic and outrageous incident of such a political alliance at public expense was the AMA's public repudiation of the Surgeon General's report in 1964, which first confirmed that smoking presented a significant health hazard. At the time, American doctors were concerned about the establishment of Medicare, fearing that it represented the first step in enacting national health insurance. The AMA solicited the votes of congressmen from mostly Southern tobacco-producing states in opposing Medicare, and in return for these votes agreed to publicly contradict the Surgeon General's report, in order to safeguard the continuing profits of the tobacco industry. The AMA did not officially express agreement with the Surgeon General's findings until more than a decade later, when the proliferation of evidence about the hazards of smoking became too overwhelming for anyone to rationally oppose. However, the power of its political lobby was displayed again more than three decades later, when the AMA successfully defeated the Clinton administration's initiatives to improve the accessibility and quality of health care for all Americans by imposing federal standards and controls.

Does all this mean that all doctors are nothing but a bunch of arrogant, mercenary despots, consumed by their own inflated self-importance and their capacity for personal enrichment? Clearly not; there are many dedicated practitioners and researchers in the medical field, obviously committed to the principles of the Hippocratic Oath and the healing of others. Yet, the extent and frequency of outrageous excesses, along with the dramatic upward spiraling of medical fees and the continual proliferation of new medical facilities, does cause one to wonder where the main priorities among the majority of the profession lie.

Western medicine's arrogance and professional myopia are evident on another level, as well. In their exclusive reliance on modern science and chemistry, which has the detrimental corollary effect of reducing the patient to a body of chemical and mechanical functions, they ignore and discount the person's capacity to use one's psychological and spiritual resources in restoring oneself to health. In fact, it is not uncommon to see doctors, in the course of "making rounds" in a hospital, speaking to the attending nurse about the patient in the third person while standing over the patient's bed, as if the patient was not a person, but an inanimate object laying there. Clearly, a view of the patient as a conglomerate of mechanical and chemical processes is not conducive to the development of good bedside manners, or of any need to do so, in the view of strictly scientifically trained doctors.

For modern medicine, the mind-body connection is largely ignored, and too often dismissed as "unscientific." Deepak Chopra recounts that his brother, a professor at Harvard Medical School, reported that over 90 percent of the doctors at that prestigious institution do not believe in the mind-body connection. Dr. Chopra asked, incredulously, "well then, how do they wiggle their toes?"

The ancient healing traditions, such as Hippocratic medicine and the Ayurvedic tradition of India, are ignored or discounted by modern medicine as "unscientific and unverifiable," and their concepts and reliance on natural processes and substances are likewise dismissed by western doctors as no more than popular superstition. Somehow, the fact that both these systems have been effectively applied for thousands of years has been conveniently overlooked by western medicine. Still, an increasing number of people are recognizing the excesses, limitations and ineffectiveness of the strict scientific approach. "Alternative medicine," widely discredited and dismissed by traditional western doctors as being without scientific basis, and therefore presumably without merit, is gaining an ever-increasing number of devotees who have been disappointed with the "take two and call me in the morning" or the "when in doubt, cut it out" approaches that so many traditional doctors rely on. The excesses, both economic and procedural, of western medicine have transformed it into a complex economic conglomerate of monstrous proportions, slowly toppling under the weight of its own excrescence and arrogance. Come to think of it, this development compares to the direction taken by our overall economy, thanks to its excessive reliance on the expenditures and priorities of the military-industrial complex.

Chiropractors, psychotherapists (not including most psychiatrists), massage therapists, herbalists, nutritionists and a wide variety of other healers are stepping in to supplant services provided by traditional doctors. The greatest collective asset of these alternative healers is that they work *with*, not *on* the person; they encourage their clients to be active in the decision-making and participation of their healing program. They recognize that a person is not a body that, just by convenient coincidence, happens to have the capacity to think and move. Rather, they regard the essential nature of human beings to be eternal spirits occupying a temporary body. The body is seen as the physical creation of that spirit, and as such, is an entity that can be altered and modified by that spirit's desires and needs. Such healers also recognize the natural processes involved in producing disease, the bodily manifestation of imbalances in emotions and feelings, and choose to restore balance in their clients' psyches and bodies in the most harmonious and least invasive manner possible. This includes counseling and the use of dietary and behavioral changes as well as natural substances, such as herbs and plant extracts, in the healing process. Alternative healers often succeed where traditional medicine has already resigned itself to failure.

Louise Hay, a pioneer in revealing the psychosomatic basis of all diseases, cured herself from cancer through a regimen of diet, meditation, prayer and counseling, after making the choice to forego any traditional treatments such as surgery or chemotherapy. More than a few of my clients with AIDS outlived pessimistic medical prognostications about their life expectancy, continuing to function normally and live vigorously far beyond their doctors' expectations, with bodies that had virtually nonexistent immune systems. One of my clients with AIDS, diagnosed as being infected with the virus as far back as 1981, was given six to nine months to live at that time. In 1992, with a t-cell (immune cell) count of 16 (about 1,000 to 1,300 is normal) he still worked 25 hours a week, played racquetball regularly, and had an active social life. He repeatedly and emphatically asserted that "this fuckin' disease ain't gonna beat me!", and I, for one, was never inclined to disagree with him!

"Miraculous" cures and recoveries have occurred in case after case where traditional medicine had given up hope of any possible recovery. They have one common characteristic: the person and his or her caretakers tapped into the human spirit's capacity to heal itself and overcome the most "hopeless" situations! Barry Neil Kaufman, the co-founder of the Option Institute in Massachusetts, has written extensively about his family's experience of healing his first son of a form of autism—a neurological disorder that medical experts regarded as permanent and irreversible. The Kaufmans' primary treatment methods consisted of daily expressions of total, unconditional love and acceptance towards this child. The boy recovered completely, and eventually revealed an exceptionally high IQ level and successfully matriculated at a very prestigious university. (The complete story is related in Mr. Kaufman's book, *Son Rise*. Well worth your time.)

In the late 1960's Dr. R. D. Laing founded a treatment center in Scotland for schizophrenics, which he named Kingsley Hall. Eschewing traditional treatment methods, such as psychotropic drugs and electroshock, and ignoring theories about chemical imbalances and genetic predisposition to schizophrenia, Laing simply included patients and staff in an environment in which there were no discernible distinctions between patients and staff in dress, function or expectations. There was simply unconditional acceptance and emotional support for everyone, no matter how extreme their behaviors or their apparent level of disturbance.

Laing regarded schizophrenia as an appropriate, if extreme, response to equally extreme life circumstances. For him, the schizophrenic experience was an odyssey within, through which the patient recovered a healthy sense of oneself. As such, it was not to be interrupted or interfered with by externally imposed antipsychotic medications or other "treatments." Although Laing never presented statistics of his results at Kingsley Hall, staff and outside researchers estimated the recovery rate of his patients to be near 90 percent, as compared to the customary recovery rates of 12 to 15 percent shown by schizophrenics subjected to traditional psychiatric treatment methods. As expected, the medical establishment quickly rose to question Laing's accomplishments and to criticize the "unscientific" nature of his work; but his unparalleled success has never been even remotely approached in traditional treatment programs.

In all these examples, and so many others, we can see the power of the human spirit to overcome any barriers and seemingly "hopeless" odds, if only it is allowed to access its full capacities. This is where modern medicine, with its exclusive reliance on science and almost total disregard of the spiritual and psychological aspects of healing, falls short. Until we return to giving our primary attention to "the ghost in the machine" and the greater Essence that is both part of us and greater than each of us, our healing efforts will remain primitive, limiting and mostly ineffective. You cannot effectively treat people in a system that has no regard for them as human beings! Included in this change to a more spiritual and personal emphasis must be the dignifying of life by also dignifying and accepting death as a natural process, one to be included in our considerations of the patient's best interests and to be accepted as a viable and even desirable alternative in the soul's evolution and development.

My own discipline, psychotherapy, also has its roots in the traditional medical model. The "father of psychoanalysis," Sigmund Freud, was a medical doctor by training, as were most of his contemporaries and disciples. Psychology and psychotherapy have only in recent decades emerged as distinct disciplines from the medical field, and in most institutional settings they are still considered to be subordinate to psychiatry—thanks to tradition, and the significant political influence of the American Medical Association lobby. Among the various types of psychotherapists—psychiatrist, psychologist, social worker, pastoral counselor, and others—psychiatrists hold the greatest power in traditional settings, and make most final decisions on treatment plans. They are also remunerated at the highest rates. Yet, they are the least extensively trained in the practice of psychotherapy of all the specialties mentioned;

psychiatrists are trained in their specialty only after completing the standard medical training all other doctors receive, and over less time than the most of the other types of psychotherapists. Moreover, much of their training is consumed with learning the possible applications of psychotropic drugs to alter affective states and control moods and behaviors. Of course, this is consistent with the medical model's view, which primarily attributes human moods and feelings to the influences of chemical processes within the body and brain. For many psychiatrists, this training and perspective results in their evolution into legal "pushers," providers of the drugs which afford to their patients temporary relief from distressing feelings without offering resolution to the life situations or behaviors associated with the origin of the distress to begin with. Thus, their patients become chronically dependent on them for relief of their discomforts, without ever evolving to more permanent alterations in their behavior patterns or affective states that might render them more self-reliant and, yes, happier.

The earlier models of psychotherapy and therapeutic institutions were also based on medical concepts, and influenced by Freudian theories. The oldest of these, psychoanalysis, required a commitment of five (six, in the earlier European model) days a week by the patient, for a period of several years. Clearly, this required a substantial financial investment, as well. One of the basic precepts of psychoanalysis emphasized the need to make the process expensive for the patient, as a key motivator for deriving maximum benefit from the process. It probably didn't hurt the analyst's motivation too much, either.

Because of the emphasis psychoanalysis placed on the earliest years of life as the time of life most receptive for the development of the various neuroses, hysterias and other dysfunctions that interfered with life satisfaction in adulthood, the minutiae of one's earliest memories, and perhaps fantasies, were examined and reexamined in tedious detail, until they could be analyzed and put in proper(?) perspective. At that point, the patient was said to be "cured." Psychoanalysis gave birth to a series of psychiatric institutions in both Europe and America, where the patients could go and examine their dysfunctions at length and in great physical comfort, while also escaping from the demands of everyday life, much as they would go to a spa. Obviously, this method of treatment was not geared to the "hoi polloi," but to the wealthy elite who could afford such an investment in money and time.

Psychoanalysis still survives today, but is no longer in the mainstream of psychotherapeutic practice. It is reserved for a dwindling minority of wealthy traditionalists, who desire and can afford such expensive and lengthy introspection. For the majority of clients, several psychotherapeutic models have been developed which provide shorter-term care (and lower cost), and mostly address current issues in the person's life, rather than lengthy examination of developmental issues dating back to childhood. Some among the traditionalists decry this development as typical of the quick-fix, immediate-gratification generation of the modern era. In truth, such an approach is the only practical alternative for resolving mental health issues at a reasonable cost, and in a timely fashion. For the majority of people seeking mental health services, a relatively short and to-the-point approach is essential, if they are to participate in therapy at all; most don't have the luxury of indulging in a leisurely and lengthy recuperation process from psychological problems before returning to functioning in the world. At a time when the stress of ordinary life is experienced by many at an unprecedented high level, and with the turning away from organized religion that has become a widening trend, psycho-therapists have become the lay priests of our society, and for many the only source of relief and opportunity for resolution of life's issues. Thus, becoming accessible to the common person has become a necessary development for most thera-pists.

However, within psychotherapy there are two divergent schools of thought, typified by their terminology for the person they're treating. One view refers to the person seeking treat-ment as the "patient," and the other as the "client." This distinction goes beyond mere semantics; it is revealing of the overall view of the person, and the philosophy of the treatment.

The first school, the one which refers to the person seeking services as the "patient," is obviously more closely related to the medical tradition of the Freudians. They take the perspective of the person as a receiver of services, more than as an equal participant in the healing process. In this framework, the therapist determines the mode and length of treatment, administers drugs when he deems it appropriate to do so, and directs the patient through self-examination and resolution of life's issues. The therapist is clearly placed in the role of the "expert," and the patient is assumed to be in a dependent and subordinate position. With few exceptions, the patient is assigned a diagnosis, which determines the direction and provides the rationale for future treatment plans, and which, not coincidentally, is necessary for obtaining insurance reimbursements. It is this therapeutic perspective that is most likely to recommend inpatient treatment (admission to a psychiatric hospital), and is most likely to be found running such programs. In such cases, treatment and administration of drugs within the hospital setting is primarily emphasized, with outpatient counseling to follow release being viewed as aftercare (an epilogue to the main, inpatient treatment).

The medically-oriented perspective is also responsible for the proliferation of prescription medications as remedies for every discomfort we experience, and every life problem that confronts us. This practice dovetails neatly with a society that has come to desire instant solutions to all its problems, and instant gratification of all its desires. It encourages the "quick-fix" of antidepressant and behavior-altering drugs, rather than the laborious and emotionally demanding process demanded by true psychotherapy. We are a society which promotes pills to wake up, sleep better, regulate appetite, control affective states, and even maintain overall health with the support and promotion of the multi-billion dollar pharmaceutical industry. Reliance on medications for regulating every aspect of daily life and maintaining "normalcy" is the desired approach for far too many among us. The price tag, however, for such artificial and ready "remedies" is steep: the further medication and consequent loss of awareness by the participants; the discouragement of self-exploration and self-awareness by individuals, further retarding their intuitive and creative impulses; the labeling and identification of those receiving the medications as "ill" or "deviant," without consideration given to the familial and societal circumstances contributing to their disturbance; and finally, the prolonged dependence and immersion of the patient on external chemical control of his/her mind and thought processes. There was ample discussion of the dire consequences of abusive and misapplied uses of prescription medications in the preceding chapter on addictions. For our discussion here, let us simply consider the number of so-called "hyperactive" children controlled by medications like Ritalin, or the millions of adults who have become dependent, at the encouragement of their doctors and families, on lithium, Valium, and Prozac, in order to even begin to appreciate the magnitude of our society's chemical abuse. Compared to the medical establishment and the pharmaceutical industry, the notorious drug cartels of Latin America look like relatively minor, "mom-and-pop" operations! There is no consideration within the medical perspective given to the recognition that the human body, among its many other wonders, is the most perfect and complete pharmacy ever created, perfectly capable of synthesizing and dispensing any substance it requires, and in the exact dosage needed.

When imbalances occur, they must be viewed and appreciated as signals of a more significant imbalance in the person's emotions and overall state. Chemical imbalances in the body are warnings of imbalances in life, and restoring order to the latter will resolve the former, without external application of drugs and pills. The externally administered restoration of chemical imbalance, without providing opportunity for the person to process and explore the conditions and circumstances for restoring the imbalance in the first place, is a violation and intrusion that interferes with true healing in the deepest, most spiritual sense. The self-healing that such complete awareness and self-exploration produces is the process behind the "spontaneous" and "miraculous" recoveries that medical science is unable to explain on its terms, and as a result discounts as "freak accidents" or "unsupported by scientific evidence." We are all capable of such deep levels of healing; the awareness of this has been kept from most of us, because it represents such a basic threat to the control the medical/pharmaceutical establishment has over our society.

The other school of therapy, the one which refers to the seeker of services as "the client," is more inclined to view that client as an active participant in the therapeutic process, an active partner who shares in the responsibility for the course and results of treatment. This perspective has evolved from the humanistic and existential philosophic traditions, and includes the cognitive therapeutic models that are so effective as short-term interventions. There is unconditional acceptance for the client as a basically healthy and viable person, separate from the problematic issue(s), and fully capable of arriving at a healthy resolution (with some help from the therapist). The therapist does not assume a superior position as an "expert," but is instead a guide, a mentor, and an assistant, a Virgil to the client's Dante.

The therapist allows the client to explore possible options through prompting, reflection and indicating, according to the client's desires and value system. This framework views confinement in institutional settings as undesirable except as a last resort, usually in cases of extreme emotional disturbance, or in the process of detoxifying the client from chemical addictions. When such inpatient intervention is indicated, therapy proper begins after release of the client from the psychiatric hospital. The client can then not only explore and resolve the relevant issues, but incorporate the resulting insights into his/her personal life as well, without the distortion of chemicals or extreme emotional upset. The therapy is very issue-specific, and relatively short in duration, so the client can go on with living life. There is very limited examination of experiences from the person's distant past, and these are only relevant for the manner in which they affect one's functioning in the present. Except for the purpose of securing insurance benefits for the client, there is no need to confine his or her experiences, issues, or identity within the boundaries of a specific psychiatric diagnosis, or to emphasize the client's "pathology" as distinct from the person.

A further word about inpatient psychiatric care: it is, in my experience, employed far more often than is actually necessary. Ideally, psychiatric confinement is best suited to persons in one of two situations: those who are so severely disturbed that they present a danger to themselves or others; and those who need a safe, restricted environment to allow addictive chemicals to eliminate from their body, so they can have full use of their thoughts and full access to their emotions during the subsequent healing process. What the general public is not always aware of is that most inpatient psychiatric facilities are financed and run much like any other business: by people whose primary motivation is profit, not optimal treatment of the patient. Often, psychiatric hospitals are run by parent corporations which own large "chains" of them—not unlike hotels, or fast-food restaurants. The administration and decision-making is primarily the province of business people and salesmen, usually with a psychiatrist nominally overseeing the medical aspect of the operation. These promoters and salespeople have monthly sales quotas, and are expected to maintain a certain steady level of income for the facility. Affiliated medical and professional staff who are not employees of the facility are expected to contribute to the patient population by referring some of their office clients for inpatient treatment. Those failing to do so in sufficient numbers find their privileges at the facility severely curtailed, or revoked altogether. It must be obvious that a person—or a facility—cannot serve two masters; where the primary emphasis is on profit, priority must clearly be given to monetary, not therapeutic, concerns. You may be sure that in most such facilities, the consulting professional contributing the greater number of patient referrals is prized significantly more than the one providing the more effective therapy. In fact, some personnel in such facilities prefer the *less* effective professionals, because incomplete or ineffective treatment means repeat business! Make no mistake about it—monetary gain is the primary motivation in all for-profit clinics and hospitals, not just the greedy few whose extreme abuses make occasional headlines, when their operations are examined by outside regulators.

Please understand: there is no stigma attached to a person who makes a handsome income by serving one's fellow man, and enriching the lives of others; quite the contrary, such a person deserves and *should* have wealth, as a natural consequence for fulfilling one's purpose in life. It is the person whose primary *motivation* comes from maximizing income that I question, because when that is the primary emphasis, quality of treatment and the patient's best interests are often compromised in the final analysis. Unfortunately, for a disturbingly large segment of the medical and psychotherapeutic profession, this shift in emphasis (along with the view of the patient as an object to be manipulated in the name of "treatment," rather than a person to be helped) has resulted in the depersonalization of the patient and a diminished capacity to deliver effective and meaningful care. It is into this gap that alternative healers and spiritual counselors have stepped to meet the need, and are transforming the nature of counseling and health care delivery along some new and decidedly non-traditional ways. I, and many other professionals, relish the improvements!

In understanding the nature and purpose of *any* disease, one basic principle must be understood: a disease has only two possible purposes for existing and manifesting in one's life, and must be understood within that context if the person is to be returned to "normal" (either in this life, or the next). Either a disease is present in order to highlight an imbalance in a person's life and psyche, which must be redressed before return to health occurs; or, it is there to provide a vehicle into the next level of existence, out of the current incarnation. How this is accomplished, and a consideration of the attendant symptoms, are all indicative of the challenge the situation presents to the person's spiritual growth, nothing more and nothing less. Once this principle is understood and more widely accepted, healing will pass completely within the province of the spiritual healer and counselor, as well as the affected person. At that point, scientific medicine, with its invasive surgical procedures and consciousness-distorting drugs, will largely pass from the healing arts. As it is, scientific medicine is mostly useful in "emergency" situations, and even here provides little insight as to the reason(s) for the condition's emergence in the patient's life. For the present, the individual needs to realize and learn to access the unlimited healing capacity that lies within each and every one of us, and which can be applied towards anything from a toothache to a tumor to pain-free delivery of a baby. True healing involves far more than the alleviating of a series of physical symptoms; a complete healing process addresses and resolves the emotional circumstances which caused the disease to emerge in the first place. Failing to achieve healing on this level will merely result in the emergence of a related set of new symptoms in the near future. As more and more people gain this awareness, the capacity to heal one's life on many levels beyond the physical will be recovered, and we will come to understand the Biblical admonition "physician, heal thyself!" as a divine invitation to us all to use the incredible healing powers within every person.

Chapter 11

The Nature and Meaning of Life

Why are we here?

Where are we going next?

What are we supposed to do while we're in this world?

These, and similar other questions, have occupied the great philosophical minds since the human race evolved beyond the focus on securing food, shelter and safety. Our society has developed along incredibly complex patterns, so that a myriad choices and opportunities present themselves to the individual. Considering the many possibilities to choose from, it's easy to feel confused and uncertain about where to focus one's energies and initiatives. As a result, some people throw themselves into acquiring wealth, others in raising a family, and still others into mastering a discipline, studying art, being accepted into high society, understanding religion, making an important contribution to mankind, or being remembered by history.

The purpose of life on earth is to provide us with learning and entertainment, contributing to the evolution of our soul. Life is eternal, but our individual lives—our incarnations—are like a flash of lightning in the sky, brief moments in eternity, small threads in the tapestry of the Divine. Any existence involving a material presence, which we call a body, a physical location (earth, or any other planet), and a continuum of time, which is a completely artificial invention of human beings, is not real. It is an illusory playground in which we can play out our fantasies and learn our lessons. This understanding puts the "tragedies" of daily life, like not getting that raise or promotion, being turned down by a prospective date, or not being approved for a Gold Card, in perspective, doesn't it? In this life, no one ever really suffers, no one really dies, and no one is ever really hurt. Even when it appears that those things occur, it is pure illusion, occurring at the invitation and with the permission of the person(s) involved. There is no more actual death, horror and tragedy in life than there is at a play or a movie. The extent to which you believe in the reality of such occurrences is the extent to which you choose to be deceived by the world's myriad delusions, and a measure of your spiritual ignorance. The same may be said of any emotional attachment to money, property, status, and titles; these are illusory trappings of the world, completely without substance.

While you are in this incarnation, you may have as much or as little of money, fame, and power as you wish. They are available in infinite supply, and you may determine and adjust the amount of each that may be included in your life, consistent with and appropriate to the roles you are currently playing. Of course, you may change your desires at any time, and the Universe will respond accordingly to your wishes. So, the apparently wealthy among us are choosing to have their wealth (along with its privileges and complications), just as the happy are choosing their happiness. Although it may not be obvious to our human eyes, or understandable to our temporal minds, the same is true of those choosing poverty, lack and tragedy. The Universe will fulfill every one of your wishes, and you are never given the capacity or opportunity to wish for anything that is beyond your grasp. Indeed, there is *nothing* beyond your grasp, and nothing you cannot manifest into or out of your life! How could there be, if your essence is divine? However, you may not be fully aware of the price for having what you want, at least on a human level. As the old saying goes, "be careful what you wish for—you just might get it!" This truism should be amended to "you *will* get it!"

While I believed in the reality of tragedy and poverty, I gave a good portion of my income to various charitable organizations, as well as to political candidates and institutions supporting those causes. This practice had three profound and readily discernible results: a) it reduced the amount of disposable income I had available to me, b) it did *not* appreciably improve the plight or reduce the numbers of the intended beneficiaries, and c) it got my name on the list of a geometrically multiplying number of charities soliciting my money for their target beneficiaries. I had not yet become consciously aware that the people whose lot in life I had attempted to improve, be they migrant workers, inner-city homeless, or potential unwed mothers, had all chosen this particular scenario as part of their lessons in this lifetime. No matter how much their human side might have sought relief from their problems, their higher spiritual self was using the seemingly distressing situation for its further enlightenment, which would have been interrupted by any "relief." I had not yet learned that what appeared to be life's "problems" were in reality gifts, with a lesson and an opportunity for soul-growth inherent in the apparent difficulties. The problem is simply the wrapping of the gift—the immediately apparent difficulty that conceals the apparent benefit(s) offered.

Stuart Wilde, the enlightened spiritual teacher, tells of the case of a soul which incarnates in order to undergo the experience of an Ethiopian youth destined to die of malnutrition and starvation at age 16. He is close to completing this experience, when suddenly the American relief vehicles appear over the horizon, laden with rice, beans and wheat. The boy's human side rejoices at the sight of his approaching rescuers, relieved at the prospect of avoiding death. However, his spiritual side despairs, because it can perceive the greater Plan at work, and can only think, "here I was almost completed with this experience, and now I'll have to hang around a few more years before I can move on."

However, I have discovered some sound reasons to return to a practice of charitable contributing of both services and money. Indeed, I have found reason to give not only of myself, but to turn my life's primary purpose towards helping to improve the lot of others. This recently acquired ideological position does not contradict my discovery that charitable contributions, for the most part, fail to appreciably alter the overall state of the person or cause they are intended to affect. Instead, it is an acknowledgment of my new awareness that, more than the contribution itself, my gift affirms to the recipients their intrinsic worth as human beings, opening the way for them to attract greater affluence to themselves beyond what any person or organization can bestow on them.

For me, the giver, there are definite benefits in the act of giving, as well. There is the affirmation that "there is more where that came from," the confirmation that I have infinite access to wealth on many levels which I am then free to share with others, and that can avail myself of the boundless joy in the giving and the reaffirming of our mutual worth. There is also the reminder that human beings are always worth more than material wealth. And finally, there is the awareness in the gesture of giving that we are all sharing the infinite bounty that is the birthright of all. These different levels of awareness, and the spirit-enhancing rewards they hold for the giver, are the benefits supporting the ancient assertion that " 'tis more blessed to give than to receive."

Back in the 1960's, we were motivated by the Kennedys, Martin Luther King, and the hippie counterculture to believe that we could transcend our parents' limitations by stepping beyond them. We thought we could transform the world through politics, through social service, through commitment to real change within our societal institutions.

We were wrong.

We learned instead that meaningful change, if it is to occur at all, must have its basis in spiritual awareness and transformation, that it happens within us, rather than around us. What we perceive as either joyous or tragic occurrences are there to motivate us, teach us, or entertain us, but in any case are no more than illusory fantasies. Because this world and everything in it are not real, there is no security in insurance, no safety in monetary savings, no permanence in institutions. We don't need any of that; we are already complete, perfect and safe, just the way we are. We are passing through our various incarnations briefly and repeatedly, and are free to choose and learn from our choices, without ever helping or hurting anyone, except in appearance—including ourselves. There are no heroes or villains, no beneficiaries or victims; but there are appearances and embodiments of these roles, and many others.

Their purpose is merely to highlight and assist our learning processes, and the appearance of contrasts seems to facilitate and accelerate this process immensely. Our spiritual growth and awareness is complete when we are able to observe these alterations and transformations in our worldly delusions with complete detachment and without even the merest trace of judgment, even when they appear to us at their most dramatic.

Each of us can make up our experience, and radically alter it as we go along. In fact, we are creating our experiences all the time, although we are not consciously aware that we are doing so. We remain within one pattern, or one level of awareness, because we find a false sense of comfort and security in familiarity. Yet, a few adventurous souls among us, recognizing that they have nothing to lose, occasionally choose to change who and where they are just to try some different experiences and get some other lessons. These are the people with the "rags to riches" stories, the geniuses, the eccentrics, the radicals, the rogues among us. Some are honored, many are feared, quite a few are vilified. But it is from and among them that the world's innovations and radical changes originate. They challenge our institutions, question our accepted beliefs, introduce new concepts, change the ways all of us live and think. These are the people who live out George Bernard Shaw's declaration that, "some people look at things as they are, and ask why; I see things that never were, and say why not?" (It is significant to me that this phrase of Shaw's became the unofficial slogan for Bobby Kennedy's 1968 presidential campaign, which began with such hope and promise, and ended so tragically. Senator Kennedy was perceived by many among the establishment of the wealthy and powerful of his time as one of the radicals and challengers to the societal status quo, one who was apparently so threatening to it that he could not be allowed to survive.)

There are great risks, if the world's opinion and acceptance of you are important, for internalizing and living by Shaw's concept; but the rewards are great, too. Don't be afraid to step out of the make-believe story of your current life, and step into a brand-new production, with a whole new cast of characters, new scenario, and different dialogue. You are not required to confine yourself to any particular future—or any particular past, for that matter. Your only real responsibility is to be true to yourself and your desires, and to pursue them. If in the process you contribute to the happiness of others, so much the better; and if you are true to yourself, you can't help but contribute to the betterment of others' lives as well. The best and most enlightened among us have been motivated by a focus on themselves and their own fulfillment. Those focusing on putting themselves and their desires aside in favor of "helping" others out of some misguided nobility or altruism have only to learn that they are squandering their opportunity to have fun and learn, and are also getting in the way of the rest of us. There is a reason why the "martyrs" and "prophets" who imposed themselves and their teachings on others uninvited were customarily stoned to death in the town square, or exiled. Imposing one's views and directives on others is not appreciated. In fact, it's downright intrusive and presumptuous—and the backlash can be dangerous! You'll learn so much more by allowing yourself the freedom to shift and change, and you'll have a lot more fun along the way. Don't worry about losing anyone along the way, either, such as your friends and family; your *real* friends and family will encourage and assist you. The others, you don't need.

Chapter 12

Envoi

The concepts and ideas that I have presented here may be new to many, and are probably contrary to the acquired perspectives from which many people view life and society. Possibly, some may have raised an eyebrow at what I've had to say; some may have scoffed, some may have become downright angry. Others may (however reluctantly) largely agree with me, perhaps recognizing in my writings some ideas and feelings they may have held for some time, but may have had difficulty articulating.

I have come to a place within myself from which the approval of others is not necessary for my self-esteem; external praise doesn't sway me, and external criticism does not dismay me. I am also unconcerned about the number of persons choosing to take a position on my work, or, for that matter, the number who bother to consider it at all. (I anticipate just a bit of good-natured disagreement from my publisher on this matter.)

My writing is intended as an offering, not as an imposition on the thoughts or emotions of others. If I have any hope for your anticipated response, it is that my work might have at least provoked you to think through—or reconsider—some of the ways in which you've come to view your world, and your place in it. If you have had cause to rethink your view(s) on a particular area, I'm pleased to have provoked that reexamination. If, after mulling the matter over, you have chosen to reject my way of thinking, that's fine with me, as well. Of course, exercising your option to never read past page six, and to decide that this volume would be put to better use in helping to cover the bottom of the canary cage or lighting the fireplace is also okay.

I make no pretense of recording any universal, all-encompassing or unshakeable truths here, although all of what I have written holds true for me. In spite of our desire to believe in their permanence and absolute nature, we actually shift and redefine our "truths" about this world constantly. Real freedom and empowerment come from the ability and willingness to always consider another point of view, a different perspective or metaphor, from the one commonly held—by yourself, or by your social milieu. Accepting and going along with ideas or institutions thoughtlessly causes a much more profound and permanent enslavement than any physical prison man has yet established, or is likely to conceive of in the future.

The great philosopher, Albert Camus, wrote that rebellion is the source of all human achievement and fulfillment. By "rebellion," Camus was not necessarily referring to the image of armed political insurrection commonly evoked by this term; he was referring to any resistance to and re-imagining of commonly-held, long-standing ideas and beliefs to which our socialization causes us to subscribe. It is on the occasions when rare individuals choose to resist such institutional and ideological tyranny, usually at great peril to themselves, that new political movements, new cultural advancements, and most important, new ideas and philosophies are engendered. The willingness to resist existing trends and rethink alternatives to the status quo was behind the Athenians' stand against overwhelming odds at Marathon; formed the basis for the teachings of Socrates and Aristotle; was behind the insurrection of the slaves led by Spartacus against Rome; Joan of Arc's campaign against the English invaders in medieval France; Martin Luther's courageous stand against the teachings and abuses of the Catholic Church; Copernicus' and Galileo's publication of their scientific findings in the face of religious censure; John Locke's treatise on the rights of man, which inspired the American and French revolutions; and even Einstein's theory of relativity, which irrevocably altered the field of physics, and led to the realization that all matter is the manifestation of consciousness and energy.

Military training and 12-step programs emphasize the K.I.S.S. rule—"keep it simple, stupid!" I have endeavored to stick closely to this principle in the process of articulating my views herein. I prefer to call it "keep it simple, sweetie," and I want to remind you of a basis for this rule which many among the military and the recovery programs may not be aware of. I'm referring to the principle that, contrary to commonly-held belief, it's not a sign of simple minds to keep one's thinking simple. It is the most brilliant minds that are able and willing to immediately "cut to the chase," and are able to decipher the bare essentials and universal truths underlying any philosophy or complex system. Simpler minds, those to whom Scott Adams refers as "in-duh-viduals," are more comfortable remaining mired in unnecessarily complex systems. This is because becoming bogged down with details and mundane functions keep them perpetually occupied, effectively preventing them from getting to the central point and the greater essence of important issues, such as the meaning of human existence. If you are doubtful about this, take the time to examine the type of person most comfortable in any such setting, like the offices of any government bureaucracy, or large corporation. Not many Einsteins in there!

Keeping it simple, and cutting through the chaff to get to the wheat of any ideological system, is the sign of a mind that doesn't waste time with wading through and being distracted by irrelevant trivialities. If you encounter someone who likes to mentally travel in ever-widening circles of obscure thoughts, you are in the presence of a person who functions best when he or she confuses and disempowers oneself and others for the purpose of controlling and manipulating them. Enlightened people are quick to recognize such persons, and give them a wide berth.

The 1960's slogan "question authority" was so empowering because, contrary to what many thought, it was not an invitation to anarchy; it was an invitation to thoroughly examine and consider the ideology and motives behind any established institution before accepting its relevance and appropriateness to the experience of each individual. Keep asking, keep questioning, keep experimenting, and most important, keep playing. *Never, ever* keep working at, or on, anyone or anything outside yourself, except to the extent that such work relates to your own voyage of self-discovery. It is important to keep marching to the beat of your own drummer, without regard for who or how many join in the parade. We were put here to play, explore, enjoy, and do our own thing, so go for it! The moments of love and pleasure we grant to ourselves and others are what make this brief passage through illusion, this instant in eternity that we call our life, worthwhile. There are only two rules for graceful—and grateful!—living, and you'll have a wonderful experience in passing through this unreal world if you'll keep your perspective and sense of humor, be willing to be unconventional and outrageous, and if you'll remember both basic rules for traveling easily and happily through this existence: "don't sweat the small stuff;" and, "it's *all* small stuff!"

Suggested Reading

Adams, Scott. *The Dilbert Future.* HarperCollins Publishers, New York, N.Y., 1997.

Bach, Richard. *Illusions.* Dell Publishing, New York, N.Y., 1977.

Bach, Richard. *Jonathan Livingston Seagull.* Avon Books, New York, N.Y., 1976.

Caldwell, Taylor. *Captains and the Kings.* Fawcett Book Group, New York, N.Y., 1983.

Chopra, Deepak. *Ageless Body, Timeless Mind.* Harmony Books, New York, N.Y., 1993.

Chopra, Deepak. *Unconditional Life.* Bantam Books, New York, N.Y., 1991.

Chopra, Deepak. *Perfect Health.* Harmony Books, New York, N.Y., 1991.

Cohen, Alan. *I Had It All the Time.* Alan Cohen Publications, Haiku, HI, 1995.

Dyer, Wayne. *Real Magic.* HarperPaperbacks, New York, N.Y., 1992.

Ellis, Albert. *How to Stubbornly Refuse to Make Yourself Miserable About Anything—Yes, Anything!* Carol Communications, New York, N.Y., 1994.

Hay, Louise. *You Can Heal Yor Life.* Hay House, Santa Monica, CA, 1984.

Kaufman, Barry Neil. *Happiness is a Choice.* Ballantine Books, New York, N.Y., 1991.

Laing, R.D. *The Politics of Experience.* Pantheon Books, New York, N.Y., 1967.

Levine, Stephen. *A Gradual Awakening.* Anchor Press, Garden City, N.Y., 1979.

Millman, Dan. *Way of the Peaceful Warrior.* H. J. Kramer, Inc., Tiburon, CA, 1980.

Rodegast, Pat, and Stanton Judith. *Emmanuel's Book, I, II, and III.* Bantam New Age Books, New York, N.Y., 1989, 1994.

Steinem, Gloria. *Revolution From Within.* Little, Brown and Co., Boston, Mass, 1992.

Walsch, Neale Donald. *Communications With God.* Putnam and Sons, New York, N.Y., 1995.

Wilde, Stuart. *Affirmations.* White Dove International, Taos, New Mexico, 1988.

Williamson, Marianne. *Illuminata.* Random House, New York, N.Y., 1994.

Index

CRAZY HORSE BOOKS

ORDER FORM

On-line orders: http://www.virtualforum.com/crazyhorse/

Postal orders: Crazy Horse Books
P. O. Box 8026
Long Island City, N.Y. 11101-8026

Please send the following books:

Qty.	Title	Price	Total
_____	*A User's Manual for Living in the World*	$22.95	_____
_____	*In the Shadow of the Scythe*	$24.95	_____

Sales Tax: Please add 8.50% for books shipped to New York State addresses.

Shipping: $4.00 for first book, $2.00 for each additional book.

Company name: _____

Name: _____

Address: _____

City: _____ State: _____ Zip: _____

Telephone: _____

Payment method: ❑ Check ❑ Cash ❑ Credit Card

Credit Card: ❑ Visa ❑ MC ❑ Amex ❑ Discover

Card number: _____

Name on card: _____ Exp. date: _____

CRAZY HORSE BOOKS

ORDER FORM

On-line orders: http://www.virtualforum.com/crazyhorse/

Postal orders: Crazy Horse Books
P. O. Box 8026
Long Island City, N.Y. 11101-8026

Please send the following books:

Qty.	Title	Price	Total
_____	*A User's Manual for Living in the World*	$22.95	_____
_____	*In the Shadow of the Scythe*	$24.95	_____

Sales Tax: Please add 8.50% for books shipped to New York State addresses.

Shipping: $4.00 for first book, $2.00 for each additional book.

Company name:_____

Name: _____

Address: _____

City:_____ State: _____Zip: _____

Telephone: _____

Payment method: ❑ Check   ❑ Cash   ❑ Credit Card

Credit Card: ❑ Visa   ❑ MC   ❑ Amex   ❑ Discover

Card number:_____

Name on card: _____ Exp. date:_____